Designing Introductory History Courses for Student Success

Designing Introductory History Courses for Student Success

edited by Julia Brookins and Laura Ansley

Published by the
American Historical Association
400 A Street SE
Washington, DC 20003
www.historians.org

© 2024 by the American Historical Association

Cover Image: David Pisnoy/Unsplash

ISBN: 978-0-87229-143-0

All rights reserved. No part of this book may be reproduced in any form without permission in writing from the publisher, except by a reviewer who wishes to quote brief passages in connection with a review written for inclusion in a magazine or newspaper.

Published in 2024 by the American Historical Association. As publisher, the American Historical Association does not adopt official views on any field of history and does not necessarily agree or disagree with the views expressed in this book.

Produced with the assistance of Brendan Gillis, Sarah Jones Weicksel, Rachel Wheatley, Elizabeth Meggyesy, and Nathan Draluck.

The application for Library of Congress Cataloging-in-Publication Data for this title has been submitted and will be available from the Library of Congress.

Table of Contents

Preface   vii
Julia Brookins and Stephanie M. Foote

Unlocking History Gateways

Many Thousands Failed: A Wakeup Call to
History Educators   3
Andrew K. Koch

Historical Thinking for Everyone   8
Kenneth Pomeranz and Anne Hyde

Introductory History Courses in 2021:
A Snapshot in Time and the Midterm View   33
Claire Vanderwood and Julia Brookins

Meeting Diverse Needs

The Unanticipated Rewards of Pedagogical Reform   49
Theresa Case

Neurodivergence and Invisible Disabilities
in the History Classroom   60
Celeste Chamberland and Michael Stelzer Jocks

Introducing History: Addressing Student Bottlenecks
While Supporting Equitable and Inclusive Learning   72
Jennifer Hart and David Pace

Two Halves of a Whole: Redesigning the US History
Survey for Relevance, Reflection, and Access   83
Sandra Frink and Margaret Rung

Themes and Variations

Building Student Engagement in History Labs   95
Elizabeth Hyde and Jonathan Mercantini

Bringing Group Research to the Large Lecture Hall   102
Kelly Hopkins

Taking a Thematic Approach with the History of Fun   110
Sara Rzeszutek

Contributors   123

Acknowledgments   127

Preface

Julia Brookins and Stephanie M. Foote

What is the value of an introductory college course in history? What are the most effective ways to train all incoming students in core elements of historical thinking? And how do we measure student success in these foundational courses? Drawing on work conducted as part of the American Historical Association's History Gateways initiative, the essays in this volume describe and document the efforts of departmental teams and individual instructors to grapple with these overarching questions at institutions across the country. The reflections and case studies that follow provide compelling evidence that thoughtful course redesign can facilitate student success in measurable ways.

With the launch of the History Gateways initiative in spring 2019, the American Historical Association led a multiyear evaluation and substantial revision of introductory college-level history courses on participating campuses across the country. Funded by a grant from the Mellon Foundation, the AHA's goal was to foster faculty-led, data-based course redesign and collaboration to support higher levels of student learning and success in lower-division history courses. Over the span of four years, faculty teams at two- and four-year colleges and universities created courses to serve students from all backgrounds and to align more effectively with the needs of a complex society.

History Gateways was born of long consideration and planning among AHA leadership and staff, with its central idea articulated in 2013 by AHA president Kenneth Pomeranz.[1] In undertaking this initiative in 2019, the AHA partnered with the John N. Gardner

---

1. Kenneth Pomeranz, "Advanced History for Beginners: Why We Should Bring What's Best about the Discipline into the Gen Ed Classroom," *Perspectives on History* 51, no. 8 (November 2013), https://www.historians.org/research-and-publications/perspectives-on-history/november-2013/advanced-history-for-beginners-why-we-should-bring-whats-best-about-the-discipline-into-the-gen-ed-classroom.

Institute for Excellence in Undergraduate Education and 11 institutional partners in three metropolitan areas: New York, Chicago, and Houston. The hope was to convene faculty members at in-person meetings in each region, and to learn from the diversity of students served by two-year, four-year, public, and private institutions.

The process and procedures for the initiative built on the Gardner Institute's Gateways to Completion (G2C) process, which had already been successful in helping institutional teams redesign lower-division courses in a wide range of disciplines across the country. History faculty members at participating institutions, with support from administrators (deans and provosts), committed to undertaking the redesign of one or two introductory history courses. They would access and review institutional data on how students performed in their courses and beyond, and assess how their courses functioned in the larger undergraduate curriculum. Together, participating faculty would discuss how students experienced their courses and consider what changes, large or small, might improve both learning and student success. Faculty themselves would conduct baseline assessments in individual course sections and make changes to the course, then collect more evidence to see what differences those changes made for students.

Some departments hoped to undertake a major redesign of their primary introductory course based on data they were eager to examine. Participants at other institutions were in a bold minority among their departmental colleagues; they had more modest plans to introduce and evaluate changes to their own course sections each time they offered the course during the project period. We envisioned a deliberative, thoughtful process that could be the centerpiece of the team members' teaching energies and attention for three years.

The focus and design of the project drew from the Gardner Institute's extensive experience in gateway course redesign work, some of which was described by Andrew K. Koch in *Perspectives on History* in 2017 (reprinted in this volume). Analysis of data on DFWI rates—the percentage of students who receive a D or F grade, who withdraw from a course, or whose progress is recorded as incomplete—revealed that an alarming number of undergraduate students were failing to progress beyond introductory history courses, an outcome that affects graduation rates for some demographic groups at even higher rates. While core college skills and historical thinking might be the focus for course instructors, "race, family income levels (based on whether a student receives a Pell Grant), gender, and status as a first-generation college student," data from the Gardner Institute illustrate, "are the best predictors of who will or will not succeed in introductory US history courses." The primary goal of the G2C process was to ensure those courses students take at the beginning of college served as openings to degree progress and future success, instead of functioning as barriers to student learning or being reasons to drop out of college. History instruction alone is not to blame for the inequities in US higher education. Rather, it might be part of a broader solution that can democratize the benefits of higher education.

Participating teams of history faculty were based at the following institutions:

New York:
Bergen Community College
Kean University
St. Francis College

Chicago:
Purdue University Northwest
Roosevelt University
University of Illinois at Chicago
Waubonsee Community College

Houston:
Houston Community College
University of Houston
University of Houston–Downtown
Texas Southern University

The COVID-19 pandemic upended many of our plans and the deliberative process of course redesign we envisioned, all but suspending the initiative's work in some contexts but also accelerating and intensifying teaching changes across many participants' courses. The lessons from this initiative, some of which are collected in this volume, reflect the variation of history faculty members' experiences during these years and a willingness to innovate thoughtfully and courageously in the midst of profound uncertainty.

This work raised a variety questions:

- There are many potential purposes for history in general education. How do you prioritize them in your designing and teaching of a single course?
- Who else has a stake in your course? How do you incorporate and balance their goals?
- Can anyone accomplish all of these goals in one term? Does it benefit your students if you try to do so? Are history faculty trying to do too much? And here, when the answer seemed to be yes, we had to ask: What are the alternatives?
- Could departments design clearly demarcated versions of introductory history courses with different sets of approaches, assignments, and assessments that are purposefully aligned to distinct skills students might need to reach their particular learning goals? What kind of faculty and advising collaboration would be needed for such a model to function well?

The initiative highlighted the need for faculty to make choices and to set teaching priorities based on their specific students and contexts. An area particularly freighted with meaning and concern for historians was reading and writing. How could instructors support students' improvement in college-level writing and reading, so central to success in higher education of any kind, while not making students' preexisting skills the determining factor in course grades?

One of the lessons from this work and from its timing was that if major collaborative redesign seems out of reach, instructors should still try incremental changes to improve student learning. Even small changes can have a significant effect on student learning and success. Attention to the needs of other stakeholders, including students as well as colleagues in other programs of study, can aid faculty members in designing and teaching a successful course. When possible, collaboration among history faculty members can make course redesign work less onerous, more effective, and more sustainable. Timely access to quality information also has an important role to play in course design: to recognize and continue making progress, instructors should be empowered with the data they need in order to see and understand how their course design and teaching choices affect students throughout their college journey. There is no one-size-fits-all way to improve student learning and success.

Along with these more programmatic and pedagogical issues, History Gateways reinforced a central intellectual challenge to history instructors. Today's college history faculty are under pressure from shifting perceptions of higher education's value. That value proposition rests in part on the benefits of college learning being spread and shared across society. Justifying the place of history in an undergraduate curriculum—but especially its place in an equitable curriculum—requires that instructors design their courses with a clear and compelling answer in mind for students who want to know why they have to take this class. For if the benefits of students' history learning are unclear, or if only certain kinds of students can derive those benefits, then the equitable thing to do is not to bother undergraduates with history requirements in general education at all. The Gardner Institute's work confronted us with statistics showing that introductory history courses derail many students from continuing toward a college degree that would be a vital asset in their quest for a better life. In light of this data, instructors and departments need to ask themselves a series of questions: Why do we offer this class, and does its design match our goals? How can it connect with students' own goals? Striving for fairness and deep learning in introductory history courses demands transparency about what is necessary to succeed in the course, and there needs to be clarity about how that success will benefit the student's development.

If they hope to design a course that communicates their essential goals transparently and engages students' own needs and ambitions fairly, history instructors must acknowledge and prioritize among the many possible purposes of an introductory history course. It is with that need in mind that esteemed historians Kenneth Pomeranz and Anne Hyde offer this volume's introductory essay: a case for disciplinary conviction as the foundation for pedagogical clarity.

Whether you are a solo faculty member teaching a single section, a departmental subcommittee adapting existing offerings, or a general education committee considering an entire undergraduate program, the introductory essay and the following contributions in this booklet can open the possibilities and imperatives of historical study as a gateway to higher learning. The breadth of approaches to course redesign in this volume's teaching reflections and case studies both demonstrates project faculty members' care in recognizing their actual students' particular needs and reveals their ingenuity in using the tools of our discipline to address them.

For the AHA and its partners, work on improving student learning and success in introductory college history courses will continue.

Unlocking History Gateways

Many Thousands Failed: A Wakeup Call to History Educators

Andrew K. Koch

This essay was originally published in Perspectives on History *in May 2017.*

In his essay "Many Thousands Gone," the 20th-century novelist and social critic James Baldwin observed, "The story of the Negro in America is the story of America—or, more precisely, it is the story of Americans. It is not a very pretty story." In the passage and the essay, Baldwin pointedly condemns how popular culture reinforces stereotypes of African Americans. But had he written the essay today, more than 60 years later, he could have just as easily been describing what is going on in introductory US history courses.

Because, in 2017, the story of African Americans enrolled in introductory US history courses is the story of the course itself. More precisely, it is the story of all students, particularly those from historically underrepresented backgrounds, who enroll in the course. And it, too, is not a pretty story. This may seem hyperbolic, but it is supported by evidence.

Over the past three years, 32 colleges and universities have worked with the nonprofit organization I serve—the John N. Gardner Institute for Excellence in Undergraduate Education—to produce a study of introductory US history courses. This analysis was conducted with the help of my colleague Brent M. Drake, the chief data officer at Purdue University and a research fellow at the Gardner Institute, who also helped with the data analysis in this article. The Gardner Institute's mission is to work with postsecondary educators to increase institutional responsibility for and outcomes associated with teaching, learning, retention, and completion. Through these efforts, the institute strives to advance higher education's larger goal of achieving equity and social justice. I had the privilege of presenting the findings as part of a preconference workshop at the 2017 AHA annual meeting.

Our data set includes outcomes for nearly 28,000 students enrolled in an introductory US history course at one of the 32 institutions during the academic years 2012–13, 2013–14, and 2014–15. These institutions included seven independent four-year institutions, six community colleges, two proprietary institutions, five public research universities, and 12 regional comprehensive public institutions, and all agreed to have their data included in the study. From the data, we sought aggregate and disaggregated rates of D, F, W (any form of withdrawal), and I (incomplete) grades in introductory US history courses. While not perfectly representative, the data allow for meaningful scrutiny of who succeeds and who fails in introductory US history courses.

The range of DFWI grades in these courses across the 32 institutions was 5.66 percent to 48.89 percent, and the average DFWI rate was 25.50 percent. This means that nearly three-quarters of all students enrolled earned a C or better. One could argue that this DFWI rate results simply from upholding standards and rigor. But troubling trends emerge upon disaggregating the same data by demographic variables—trends that may very well reveal that the term "rigor" enables institutionalized inequity to persist.

Race, family income levels (based on whether a student receives a Pell Grant), gender, and status as a first-generation college student are the best predictors of who will or will not succeed in introductory US history courses. As Table 1 shows, the likelihood of earning a D, F, W, or I grade is lower for Asian American, white, and female students who are not first generation and do not receive a Pell Grant. It is higher, sometimes significantly higher, for every other demographic group.

Some see failing a course as beneficial: it can be a reality check that helps students learn what is necessary to succeed in college and may even help point toward programs for which they are "better suited." The problem with that consoling argument is the fact that for some students, failure in even one course such as introductory US history predicts ultimate dropout from college altogether.

Institutional dropout rates show that the students who took introductory US history, were otherwise in overall good academic standing, and opted not to return to the institution the following

Table 1. Rates of D, F, W, or I grades in introductory US history by demographic group

Demographic Group	DFWI Rate (%)
Asian American	17.37
White	21.36
Not first generation	22.14
Not Pell Grant recipient	22.65
Female	22.67
Course Average	*25.50*
First generation	26.13
Male	27.18
Nonresident alien	28.26
Pell Grant recipient	28.49
Two or more races	31.42
Hispanic/Latino	32.85
American Indian/Alaska Native	40.51
Native Hawaiian/other Pacific Islander	41.73
African American/Black	42.37

year were over twice as likely to have earned a D, F, W, or I in the course (42.87 percent) than retained students in good academic standing (19.27 percent). Failure in the course, therefore, was not necessarily an indicator of being a bad student—because these students were otherwise in good academic standing—but was directly correlated with students' departure decisions. Adding to these disturbing data are two national studies that show that college students who do not succeed in even one of their foundational-level courses are the least likely to complete a degree at any institution over the 11-year period covered by the studies.[1]

---

1. Clifford Adelman, *Answers in the Toolbox: Academic Intensity, Attendance Patterns, and Bachelor's Degree Attainment*, Office of Educational Research and Improvement (US Department of Education, 1999), https://www2.ed.gov/pubs/Toolbox/toolbox.html; Adelman, *The Toolbox Revisited: Paths to Degree Completion from High School through College*, Office of Educational Research and Improvement (US Department of Education, 2006), https://www2.ed.gov/rschstat/research/pubs/toolboxrevisit/.

When one considers the characteristics of students who are more likely to earn a D, F, W, or I in an introductory history course alongside the retention and completion implications, it is clear that there is a problem. And this problem is that many well-established approaches to teaching introductory history and other foundational college courses may be subtly but effectively promoting inequity.

This ugly picture can only get worse if teachers and professionals charged with supporting enrolled students continue with a business-as-usual approach. According to the Western Interstate Commission of Higher Education's report *Knocking at the College Door*, high school graduating class sizes are shrinking. At the same time, the very same populations that are least likely to enroll and succeed in college—underrepresented minority, first-generation, and low-income students—will constitute larger percentages of high school graduates and beginning college students.[2] While they might not lack the cognitive wherewithal to learn and succeed, they often lack the cultural capital and sense of social belonging their more advantaged counterparts possess. A single failure can confirm preexisting attitudes that "I'm just not college material" or that "I don't belong here."

But there is hope: methods and means that can help counter these trends. Such methods include increasing expectations for our students, engaging with them, and directing them to available academic support.

Our knowledge about what works in postsecondary teaching and learning has advanced significantly since the end of the 20th century. New approaches include the use of evidence-based, active-learning strategies in college courses of various sizes. These strategies improve outcomes for all students, especially those from the least advantaged backgrounds.[3] Also showing

---

2. Brian T. Prescott and Peace Bransberger, *Knocking at the College Door: Projections of High School Graduates* (Western Interstate Commission for Higher Education, 2012). For more information and contemporary reports, see http://knocking.wiche.edu/.

3. Scott Freeman, Sarah L. Eddy, Miles McDonough, Michelle K. Smith, Nnadozie Okoroafor, Hannah Jordt, and Mary Pat Wenderoth, "Active Learning Increases Student Performance in Science, Engineering, and Mathematics," *Proceedings of the National Academy of Sciences* 111, no. 23 (2014): 8410–15. J. Patrick McCarthy and Liam Anderson, "Active Learning Techniques versus Traditional Teaching Styles: Two Experiments from History and Political Science," *Innovative Higher Education* 24, no. 4 (2000): 279–94.

great promise is the use of embedded (therefore required) support for all students—since, as the higher education researcher Kay McClenny notes, "at-risk students don't do optional."[4] And providing early and frequent feedback in courses—increasingly by using predictive analytics and intervention mechanisms—also has benefits.[5]

So now that you know this, what will you do? Will you examine data from your institution to see whether comparable trends exist in the courses you teach? If you find them, will you explore the resources available to you and use them to redesign your courses—both their structure and the way you teach them? Will you reach out to students? Will you explore professional development activities provided through your institution's center for teaching excellence or through entities like the American Historical Association's Teaching Division or the International Society for the Scholarship of Teaching and Learning in History?

In an era of "alternative facts" and "extreme vetting," it is easy to feel powerless. But the issues in introductory history courses—a form of vetting, too—existed long before the atmosphere following the 2016 election. That is not an alternative fact. If inequity in the United States concerns you, and inequitable outcomes exist in the courses you and your colleagues teach, then it is important to remember that you have agency to address this.

As historians, we know that we are agents of history acting in history to shape it. Therefore, I encourage you to shape history by reshaping the history courses you teach. In the process, you may very well be creating a much more hopeful and "prettier" story.

---

4. Jim Henry, Holly Bruland, and Jennifer Sano-Franchini, "Course-Embedded Mentoring for First-Year Students: Melding Academic Subject Support with Role Modeling, Psycho-Social Support, and Goal Setting—TA," *International Journal for the Scholarship of Teaching and Learning* 5, no. 2, article 16 (2011): 1–22, https://doi.org/10.20429/ijsotl.2011.050216.

5. Kimberly E. Arnold and Matthew D. Pistilli, "Course Signals at Purdue: Using Learning Analytics to Increase Student Success," in *Proceedings of the 2nd International Conference on Learning Analytics and Knowledge* (ACM, 2012), 267–70.

Historical Thinking for Everyone

Kenneth Pomeranz and Anne Hyde

Everything has a history, including the discipline of history itself—especially its position in our places of learning and public culture. Nonetheless, developments took some surprising turns over the last decade. There were certainly warnings: some state legislatures and many local officials aimed to commemorate their own versions of the past and claimed that efforts to revise histories to include a broader range of participants posed a danger to stability, public order, and patriotism. While some voices insisted that history was dead—irrelevant to college education, to civic discussion, and to students' postcollegiate lives—even more saw it as dangerous propaganda. Few of those debates paid attention to how history courses are designed or taught—our concern here. History remains essential to general education requirements not primarily because students learn specific facts, but because they learn skills fundamental to college and life.

A number of recent trends—including the turn after 2008 toward "practical" majors and increasingly vociferous attacks on non-STEM higher ed (especially at public institutions)—have persuaded many historians of the need to articulate more clearly and forcefully the benefits of historical education and a history major.[1] The AHA's Tuning the History Discipline initiative, which began in 2011, is a good example of a sustained, coordinated effort to do this. And there is no more important place to explain the value of thinking like a historian than in our introductory courses.

---

1. Robert B. Townsend, "Data Show a Decline in History Majors," *Perspectives on History* 51, no. 4 (April 2013), https://www.historians.org/publications-and-directories/perspectives-on-history/april-2013/data-show-a-decline-in-history-majors; Benjamin M. Schmidt, "The History BA since the Great Recession," *Perspectives on History* 56, no. 9 (December 2018), https://www.historians.org/research-and-publications/perspectives-on-history/december-2018/the-history-ba-since-the-great-recession-the-2018-aha-majors-report.

The need to be clear about what history is good for, ironically, has been fed also by the progress of our field. Recent decades have seen a vast expansion in the range of history offerings, as courses once narrowly focused on the West added histories from around the world, from more diverse groups within the West, and even of nonhuman and environmental topics. That far-ranging growth in human knowledge—itself an undoubtedly good thing—makes it more difficult to anchor history's significance in a single set of facts about the past that "everyone" should know. Should an introductory course be a broad survey, or should it focus on topics that speak directly to students' present concerns? Without a consensus on the necessity of grasping any particular set of facts, enumerating the skills and mental habits that history teaches is vital.

This essay describes and reasserts the importance of learning to think like historians. History is unlikely to retain its place in general education requirements if we don't do a better job articulating what it offers to people in their current and future roles as community members, parents, workers, and voters. A broad directive, thinking like a historian includes interrogating facts and adding context to clarify the significance of details; developing an analytical process of reading and questioning that tests an author's claims and evidence; and building arguments from imperfect materials—arguments that are provisional, editable, and not unquestionably true, but that are demonstrably more convincing than other available arguments about the same topic. Once described and practiced, those tools and basic habits of mind will be useful to every college student faced with managing a digital world sending out torrents of images and words.

From there, this essay suggests ways to teach these skills and modes of thought in a general introductory course. We don't have a magic formula, and we offer these ideas as a way to spark discussion about best methods. We hope readers will test our claims and add their own experiences and observations. We acknowledge from the start that much of what we propose requires "slow thinking," teaching skills of critical inquiry, contextualization, and close reading. But we are convinced that focusing on less can in fact yield more. As historians of China and the United States, our examples reflect those specific experiences, but our choices demonstrate how historical thinking can empower every college student's questions and aspirations. Students come to the classroom embedded in cultures and communities, and they need to ask big questions: Who am I and how did I get here? How am I, and my world, changing? What does it mean to be human? Do I see the world in the same way as other people? Why and how do leaders, parents, and peers make their decisions? What is a fact? What is an interpretation? What can I count on?

None of this is easy. Historians know and should demonstrate that facts have meaning only in context. To recognize that Kaifeng had 900,000 or more people in 1100 CE is to know a piece of trivia obtainable by anyone with an internet connection. But to have historical knowledge is to understand what made a city of that size sustainable in an era before steam-powered transportation, how people were organized to distribute work, food, and status and to maintain public order, what kinds of cultural mixing occurred, why the city's population fell to 90,000 by 1330, and how modern scholars have understood the significance of this spectacular efflorescence and its collapse—for China, the dynamics of urbanization, the significance of fossil fuels (Kaifeng burned lots of coal, mostly to make iron), and more.

More controversially, for US citizens to know exactly what Lincoln said at Cooper Union about slavery and national unity, or for them to know how many people died in the bombing of Hiroshima (compared with how many were expected to die in an invasion of Japan), will not provide them with a final answer to any important question. But these pieces of information can advance larger discussions about how slavery seeded itself in US culture, or why so many people now view "precision" bombing in urban areas as a routine tool of warfare.

What does this mean for students who take only one college-level history course? And what does it mean for our introductory courses—not always surveys—that begin the process of teaching majors to master historical thinking while simultaneously helping nonmajors gain some measure of those skills? What are the best ways to make that happen? Equally important, how do we make these courses attractive to students (and their advisors) who are choosing from among many possible ways to fulfill distribution requirements?

Put another way: What do we, as historians, have to offer? Clearly, our own disciplinary undergirding can be seen here in the questions by which we proceed and the provisional nature of our claims. We are not sure and, actually, we don't want our students to be sure. Writing and educating with more uncertainty than authority is the key to teaching students to *analyze*, a term we use loosely but activate with precision. First, we ask questions in particular ways. Such questions are the opening moves toward analysis, which comes from the Greek word for "breaking apart." So we start with *description*: What happened? If an event began because of a single cause, why do different people explain what happened in different ways? Then, *analysis*: Why did it happen? Why do we think that? Then, *argument*: What do I think? What is my evidence and where did it come from? Finally, *implications*: If my argument is (provisionally) valid for this case, are there other cases or general relationships—in either the past or the present—that should be reconsidered in that light?

Our epistemology demands making a tentative case about truth using evidence that is always limited. A historian may believe that their claim makes more sense than another because it is more consistent with a known body of evidence and with patterns observed in other cases. But they also know that with more data, or with different ways of looking at the original data, their claim could change. This is hard to do, to explain, and to teach. Testing claims is conversational, relational, and never absolute. It leaves instructors and their students on somewhat shaky ground. Students must be persuaded to test ideas they aren't sure of—and even more vitally, ideas they are absolutely certain about—just as historians are willing to have their claims corrected and improved as new perspectives and data are considered. We need to share the fact that our thinking evolves out loud, in class: "I used to know this, but now I think this, and here's why." In a 2015 article, Josh Ashenmiller laid out the core of his teaching goals. He wanted "students to sit in front of a keyboard paralyzed by doubt, struggling with epistemological questions, 'How do I really know what happened? And, what exactly is a fact?'" Ashenmiller expressed a hope for his students that we probably all share: "I want them forever to question what is or was inevitable."[2]

This goal is crucial. Forcing students to slow down and consider how they make decisions, and to consider where information

---

2. Josh Ashenmiller, "SLO Curve Ball: What I Really Want for My Students," *Perspectives on History* 53, no. 1 (January 2015), https://www.historians.org/research-and-publications/perspectives-on-history/january-2015/slo-curve-ball.

came from, has utility far beyond the classroom. The rhetorical moves used by historians give people the tools and patience to listen to each other, which is vital for civic conversation. With luck, these approaches generate arguments striking enough to give those we disagree with pause, and encourage them to suspend their own certainty and to listen. Consider this set of rhetorical steps that enable us to talk and to disagree: "Here is what I think now, and the evidence suggests that my claim here is true." But, and this is key, "I know that I never have all the evidence, so new evidence could change my mind." Then, "What do *you* think?" We use conversational moves to arouse someone's interest and link it to ours. Such a conversational mode is vital to teaching the rhetoric of argument and the steps by which historians present evidence to support our points.

[Margin note: An idealized, platonic version - has it ever been true?]

The historian's particular toolkit is honed by the way we read and the unusual variety of materials we use. We sometimes take that range for granted, but we should highlight how our work differs from experts whose range of materials is often narrower, their methods used in less skeptical ways. Our tools allow us to read materials designed to advocate for a particular viewpoint (blogs, legal briefs, private letters) and materials that were written for different purposes entirely (census data, shipping manifests, school curricula, cookbooks). When we pull those materials into the present, we use them for purposes very different from those for which they were written. Our method reads materials both for what they might tell us about a more or less objective reality (as a set of rent receipts tells us what housing cost in a specific time and place) and for what they might tell us about the minds of the people who wrote and read them. The instructor of a 20th-century history course might assign excerpts from Adolf Hitler's *Mein Kampf*, but not because they believe that it imparts objective truths about the workings of capitalism, the reason Germany lost World War I, or anything else. Instead, we read it to understand something about the people who found its dangerous claims persuasive.

Of course, texts don't come to us prelabeled, with instructions to "read this for what it tells you about the external world" or "read this only for what it tells you about the minds of its authors or audience." But teaching students to read documents requires being crystal clear about different goals: What does the text say? And how can we use context to understand its meaning? That is as true of online materials as it is of historical documents. What history can teach you is how to decide which materials are useful for what kinds of questions, and how to read them. Most materials can be read in more than one way—and should be. A census, for instance, claims to provide objective information about an external world: How many people lived in Rio de Janeiro in 1880? In 1980? However, confirming that it does so requires going beyond the document itself: What can we find out about how this census was conducted, and how reliable are its numbers? Meanwhile, whatever we conclude about the census' quantitative accuracy, we can also read it to reveal the minds of its designers: Why did they have this set of ethnic categories in that era? Why was this question asked only to men or to women? How did they assess the respondents' literacy?

We also read "documents" that aren't documents at all: potsherds, tree rings, buildings, statues, clothing. And reading is not the same as looking; there are things we have to learn to do in order to use these sources, and it is important that our students understand this. Often, it's a matter of learning special skills from another discipline. We can turn tree rings into data about an area and era's rainfall, temperature, and other environmental conditions; we can also use the changing numbers of Chinese ceramic fragments in different layers of an East African archaeological site to explore transformations in trade, luxury consumption, or class divisions. Sometimes what we need most is not a special skill but simply the open-mindedness to see something that is plainly there but contradicts our expectations.

In his 2002 book *Historical Thinking and Other Unnatural Acts*, education scholar Sam Wineburg gives us an excellent example of how not to take this last kind of seeing for granted, and how going back and forth between an image and our other knowledge and opinions about an event it portrays can further the particular goals of historical thinking. A class of high school students was given several accounts of the Battle of Lexington, an event widely celebrated as the moment when the first shots of the American Revolution were fired. That understanding of the event is in many ways quite logical. But a mythic version of this moment of national origin is so strongly embedded in the minds of even young Americans that it can blind us to what actually happened. In this case, only one student noticed that the accounts from 1775 did not describe a battle between two roughly comparable armies; instead, they made it clear that a company of trained British regulars had lopsidedly defeated a hopelessly outnumbered, outgunned, and inexperienced group of hastily assembled colonists.[3] We will return to this example later; what matters now is that this student's insight was rare not because it required either technical proficiency or deep knowledge of the period. Seeing struggle rather than triumph required the historian's capacity to notice how new evidence—new to these students, at least—required modifying a generally accepted narrative. In showing this student new evidence about an event, the exercise not only changed his mind about that event but opened up questions about something that happened later (and is, in fact, still ongoing): the reinterpretation and mythologizing of the American Revolution.

In some cases, historians can learn crucial things about the past even from the *absence* of documents. This must be done cautiously and only when we are confident that people ignored something in their world that we consider important; it is not for when evidence of their awareness might well have been lost. For example, what do we make of the fact that observers who wrote about their overland trail experience in the mid-19th-century United States never noted Black travelers? We know from census records that thousands of enslaved people were moved west by their enslavers and from property records that hundreds more freed themselves and migrated to California and Oregon. Why did these Black travelers remain otherwise invisible in the record?

Both history and life are about making decisions from flawed evidence. Raising doubts and acknowledging uncertainty is a stance that has both analytical and ethical power. In introductory classes, many students struggle with the dread of being wrong, fearful that it might prove they don't belong in college. Consequently, they rarely answer questions or ask for help, and they don't read the syllabus carefully. Testing ideas in public is scary. Learning requires making mistakes and trying again—impossible terrain for some students. With its giant store of examples of past human actions and folly (decisions made in which students have no obvious personal stake), history classes offer the perfect place to practice. We can tell students that if they're not sure they're

---

3. Sam Wineburg, *Historical Thinking and Other Unnatural Acts* (Temple University Press, 2001), 8–10, 67–69.

right, they're quite likely headed in the right direction. Wrestling with complexity and doubting single explanations is a useful way of navigating the world, and we should be evangelists in sharing how historians' particular skepticism works.

This is tricky. First, students don't come to college history courses with no knowledge (though they sometimes think they do). It is our job to persuade them that we offer a procedure for acquiring and validating knowledge, not just one more opinion that is no better or worse than those they may have gotten from Hollywood, websites, their Uncle Fred, or a randomly selected textbook. We are developing a critical habit of uncertainty to test *all* opinions, including our own. If we do this well, students will find arguing about historical interpretation genuinely exciting, and it will become an important part of growing beyond the constraints of their own pasts. Seeing a bigger world and providing tools for analyzing it is vital in helping people understand the stakes involved in debating history, and the necessity of doing so. That process can shape habits of critical thinking (by which we mean taking apart claims, assessing evidence, and doubting that any result is final) that go beyond our classrooms and matter regardless of what the student chooses for a major and a career.

Second, much as we may regret it, certain kinds of arguments for studying history that are based on the idea that all citizens should possess a certain body of knowledge—e.g., all Americans should know why there are two Koreas or why the federal government owns so much land out west (and what it does with that land)—don't have the traction they once did, particularly for students who are pessimistic about the value of political participation. Is some such knowledge essential? Shouldn't everybody know what has happened to energy consumption, synthetic nitrogen production, and extinction rates over the last hundred years? To crime, incarceration, and gun-ownership rates? To how many hours different kinds of people have spent "working" over the last 500 years? (Not to mention that it's still worthwhile to know why there are two Koreas.) But we cannot make students retain such knowledge beyond their final exams—much less get them in the habit of updating it—simply by digging in our heels about what everyone "should know." Instead, an important goal of introductory courses should be to persuade students that some facts are important not *although* they are historical (that is, about the past rather than the present), but *because* they are historical. Since past and present are always intertwined, these particular facts can either sustain or undermine widely believed "commonsense" narratives about the past that powerfully shape how we navigate the present.

   This is not to suggest that the introductory course should take its charge from the frequently published surveys that conclude Americans know "nothing" about history and rush to fill this presumed void of knowledge with some minimal set of facts. Rather, our approach to teaching insists that even beginning students do "know" some history. Some of what they know—or find, if they search online—is reasonably accurate; some of it is inaccurate and even dangerous. Much knowledge is so taken for granted that students might never have considered that what they regard as knowledge is in fact a set of claims. Consider how many students "know" without thinking that all cowboys were white, that the US military played the major role in defeating Nazism, that modern societies are more accepting of same-sex relationships than were premodern societies, and that we have far more leisure time than our ancestors did. Convincing students that they have such beliefs, often implicit, is a core task. Unearthing and challenging such ideas without making students feel defensive about having them is delicate, ongoing work.

   That work can proceed along a range of creative pathways. One strategy is to have students reveal their own implicit knowledge through an innocent exercise. Students in intro US history courses generally acknowledge having little knowledge of colonial North America but also deny wearing any significant blinders on the topic. To show them otherwise gently, one former colleague regularly started her early US history survey by asking every student to draw "a colonial American"—a simple stick figure would suffice. An astonishing percentage of her students drew a man (or occasionally a woman) in a Pilgrim costume; almost none drew an African or a Native American, or even a white person marked as coming from a different colonial community. Contrasting their drawings with the demographic reality—that Pilgrims were but a small percentage of the colonial population—was her way to show students that they do indeed carry historical narratives with them, and that those narratives matter to questions as basic as who a US history course is about and who a "real American" is today.

There are many ways to begin the slow process of raising awareness and sowing doubt about what constitutes "common knowledge." Sometimes, picking apart somebody else's common knowledge can become a toehold from which to challenge our own. For instance, almost all history textbooks published in the People's Republic of China contain a sentence like: "On September 2, 1945, the Chinese people's eight-year struggle against Japanese imperialist invaders came to a triumphant end." Most American students can grasp that this statement is technically true but badly misleading, as it omits the central role of the United States and other allies in forcing the Japanese empire to surrender. The payoff for American students comes when you then seed doubt about our own country's widely accepted narrative about World War II in Europe: that the United States, perhaps with the help of Great Britain, defeated the Nazis. That, of course, is as partial a truth as its Chinese counterpart, since the vast majority of Nazi casualties were inflicted by the Soviet Union. Belief in our own misleading half-truth owes more to the efforts of Hollywood than to the government's imposition of a party line on textbooks, as occurs in China. That difference is worth noting because it can lead to a productive discussion of the many ways that ideology is generated and reproduced. But those differences do not obviate the central point of using Chinese half-truths about World War II to set up an inquiry into American beliefs: that while Americans may live in a society in which bad historical ideas can be challenged much more easily than in China, many of us still "know" a good deal of distorted history, often without realizing it. Moreover, these distortions inevitably affect debates about contemporary affairs, favoring some positions at the expense of others.

Some students find it easier to accept that they hold misleading beliefs if we can show how such ideas become embedded in cultural memory, often transferred to us when we are far too young to see what is happening. Working on a world history textbook, one of us surveyed a number of world maps designed for children (as jigsaw puzzles, for instance). In every map, Europe was illustrated with iconic buildings (the Eiffel Tower, Big Ben, the Roman Colosseum); animals were rare except at the margins of the continent (a bull in Spain, a reindeer in northern Scandinavia). On the same maps, Africa was almost exclusively represented by wild animals (lions, elephants, zebras); the only buildings were, once again, at the edges (a pyramid or a sphinx in Egypt, often considered part of the Middle East rather than Africa). The rest of the world is depicted with a more even mix of icons: South Asia, for instance, is almost always marked by the Taj Mahal and an elephant. It is easy to see that such imagery will inculcate in children a semiconscious association of Europeans with "culture" and Africans with "nature" (with the rest of the world on a continuum in between)—an association not necessarily dislodged by learning that today Africa is the home to several of the world's largest cities, or that people without cities and monumental buildings nonetheless left unmistakable proof in art and on the landscape that they had "culture." You could pair the example of children's maps with photographic portrayals from *National Geographic* of Native Americans, Indigenous Pacific Islanders, and Africans, which match perceptions the magazine's readers developed in childhood. Finally, one can link that association backward to 19th-century theories of racial difference, which few people today admit to tolerating, thereby showing that ideas which have been discredited intellectually can nonetheless persist in popular culture if we do not make the effort to interrogate that culture with the same critical eye that we use for scholarly debates. One can then link the same association of some people with nature and others with culture to unacknowledged beliefs that often color contemporary debates.

By contrast, simply telling students about 19th-century racial theorizing before suggesting that subtle influences of these ideas linger today will prompt few of them to interrogate contemporary attitudes. Pointing to a concrete mechanism for transmission of these ideas—such as children's maps or what pops up on Wikipedia—makes the claim more convincing. And since nobody expects small children to be especially critical of what they're shown, highlighting these mechanisms helps avoid a defense that amounts to "I'm too smart/aware/decent a person of the present to be influenced by those bad old ideas." We all face challenges in our classrooms while laying out pieces of the past that do harm in the present. This defensive response often recedes as people develop the capacity to contextualize historical events, analyze historical continuity, and identify the difference between structure and agency. Breaking down this defensiveness must begin somewhere: demonstrating how popular culture turns bad history into "common sense," before we are even aware it's happened, is one way to start.

By foregrounding the uprooting of "common sense," we also highlight the importance of our discipline *as a discipline*—a vital task precisely because it tends to remain hidden when we lean on narrative and facts. The natural sciences have clear and identifiable methods that are distinct from simply thinking: experiments, equations, modeling. Some social sciences—particularly the more quantitative branches—also showcase their methods, and introductions to those fields often begin by laying out their assumptions. Even assumptions historians see as profoundly limiting—the "rational actor" models beloved by economists and some political scientists, say—can, when made explicit, demonstrate the merits of stating one's ideas up front and send a powerful signal to introductory students: "What we do in this class has a method that you have to learn, and not just by osmosis."

That message of disciplinary value is reinforced whenever a discipline demonstrates something counterintuitive: that the flat earth beneath our feet is round and rapidly moving, or that rent control can actually hurt renters. By contrast, introductions to history often jump straight into telling a story, with no prior discussion of methods or assumptions. Indeed, most textbooks start their narratives on page 1 and rarely interrupt them with questions of method or alternative views. In order to create a smooth narrative, they obscure both the processes by which historians have settled on the stories they tell and the likelihood that today's consensus was not the consensus of historians a generation ago. But smoothness, like speed, is rarely good for critical thinking. When we write for each other, historians not only leave the bumps in but often focus on them.

This is no accident: it is a key insight into the historian's method. We expect our colleagues to take us more seriously when we admit that intellectually respectable people can disagree with one another's claims; indeed, an author's own disagreement with widely held views is often central to their pitch for why their contribution is worth reading. Making that pitch frequently involves an explicit discussion of method, as when historians point out that other scholars have relied on biased sources, failed to look at evidence that we deem relevant, or based their argument on an "average" resident of a specific time and place without considering how residents of different classes, races, genders, and ages might have experienced the same events.

This question of disparate, even contradictory, sources and subjects points not only to hazards ahead but to possibilities worth teaching, and to another arrow in our professional quiver: a range of reading techniques. We tend to read texts in many ways rather than limiting ourselves to a single approach. Sometimes, for instance, we read like philosophers, looking to reconstruct the logic of an argument. But unlike philosophers, we don't lose interest in the text if it fails a logical test or focus on determining how that failure might be remedied; instead, we're more likely to ask why a particular set of readers didn't notice or care about a flaw that we can see. Similarly, sometimes we read like literary critics, asking how a text achieved certain effects for a certain audience—but we're also interested in whether and how its claims mirrored what other evidence tells us was "really" going on. This eclecticism not only teaches students different ways to read; it predisposes them to finding different things, to seeing long-settled landscapes from exciting new angles.

Historians read a variety of materials with a distinctive set of tools: so far, so good. But they also sharpen another skill worth emphasizing: the use of *context* for understanding a people, document, or event. Sometimes we are interested in a text that said something unusual for its time and place—as do most texts studied by other humanists (Aristotle, Ibn Khaldun, and Virginia Woolf were hardly "typical"). Other times, less original thinkers are the most useful for our purposes, precisely because we know that many of their contemporaries had similar ideas. Another comparative move and critical skill is juxtaposing things to other things of their time—so one might ask how British women's magazines from the 1910s compare to Virginia Woolf's first novel. Using comparative context also helps eliminate certain meanings that have been falsely attributed to ideas by taking them out of context, such as various "intents" imputed to the authors of the US Constitution.

Consequently, though we know that treating a society as a holistic and independent unit is to partake in a fiction, we also believe there is much to be learned by repositioning the things we are curious about next to others from roughly the same time and place. There is no self-contained unit called "France," moving through time, internally homogeneous and neatly separable from others called "Germany" or "Haiti." In fact, the fiction of self-evident national units with a single history is among the most troublesome narrative devices used by historians, particularly in our current political moment. But even if we don't believe in a neat unit called "19th-century France," there is value in reconstructing a context that included a rapidly falling birth rate, struggles over secular education, the colonization of Algeria, and the dawn of impressionism—and in seeing how comparison makes each of these elements look different from how it would in isolation. After all, people living in 19th-century France would have been touched by all these things; they would have argued about the proper role of the Catholic Church while being aware that the birth rate was falling and vice versa.

Moreover, one rarely knows in advance which context will prove most helpful to understanding one's subject. This is an argument for casting our nets widely, for including impressionists, farm wives, and Algerian colonists in our demarcation of "19th-century France." Let us return for a moment to Wineburg's experience teaching the Battle of Lexington. The thoughtful student who noticed that the accounts were of a one-sided massacre, not an evenly pitched battle, was then asked (along with the rest of the class) to choose from several pictures of the event the one he thought was probably most accurate. Knowing one part of the context—that the colonists were badly disadvantaged in both weaponry and training—and assuming that they were not stupid, the student chose a picture that showed the colonists fighting a guerrilla war: hiding as much as they could and sniping at the British from behind walls and trees, rather than confronting them directly. This, indeed, is precisely what many colonial fighters *eventually* did, but that did not happen at Lexington. There, the colonists tried to fight head on and paid dearly. This was not because they were stupid—the student was correct about that—and we should encourage other students to avoid condescension toward those we study, invoking "stupidity" only as a last resort, even when historical actors seem to have missed something that is obvious to us. (This, too, is a lesson from historical reasoning that has much to offer in the present, as we struggle to understand the contemporaries with whom we most strongly disagree.)

What Wineburg's student didn't know—but might learn by the end of a well-rounded survey of early America—is that guerrilla tactics violated contemporary standards of masculinity: "honorable" men didn't fight in such "cowardly" ways, so it took time for the colonists to accept that they would need to do so to survive (and thereby uphold other values they cherished). That the answer to a puzzle about military tactics requires some knowledge of the period's gender norms—often regarded a soft or innovative topic, remote from hard, old-fashioned military history—demonstrates the importance of broad contextualization, reconstructing many aspects of people's lives as a strategy for historical understanding. To add still another dimension to this context, many colonists associated guerrilla tactics with Native Americans, making racial ideologies also relevant to Lexington and its aftermath.

This analysis of American Revolutionary warfare must rely heavily on inference. Historians can find documents from this period in which people discuss the norms of fair fighting among honest men, and they can reasonably argue that the men at Lexington had absorbed such views. They can even show cases in which such norms influenced the behavior of soldiers on both sides of the conflict—a related act of self-restraint by a British officer may well have saved George Washington's life in 1777. But we are unlikely to find a source in which a Lexington survivor said explicitly that "we fought out in the open because it was the manly thing to do, and we wanted to be manly." Working through such examples from start to finish can help students see the difference between being "dumb" and sharing the "common sense" of one's community, even when that sense has the deadly effect of making people miss opportunities (or dangers) that outsiders like ourselves see plainly. It also shows, again, that we can sometimes get into a historical subject's head by noting what they did *not* say or do and trying to determine why it didn't occur to them or why they saw no need to mention it. But we can never do so with complete confidence: nobody tells us directly what they *weren't* considering, much less why.

So comparison, critical reading, context, and skepticism enable historians and our students to consider big, important questions by using specific cases. What causes change—climate, human decisions, technology, or fate? Why did so many people uproot, migrate, or rebel in the era between 1300 and 1700? Why did many of their contemporaries stay put? When the Little Ice Age affected regions across the Northern Hemisphere, why did some people and communities adapt while others did not? Here we can broaden our inquiry to other environmentally induced crises: Did places like Chaco Canyon, Cahokia, Greenland, or Tenochtitlan fall or merely change? For centuries, most educated people in the West (and many elsewhere) have "known" that Rome "fell" in the late 400s, and they have piles of written material to prove it. Yet more recently, scholars have argued that while the end of the western Roman empire *as an empire* caused great losses to urban elites (who wrote most of our sources), it is quite possible that ordinary people (especially those living in the countryside) benefited so significantly from the inability of that same elite to collect taxes and rents that it canceled out any losses from increased disorder, disruptions of trade, and so on. The same is true for the roughly contemporaneous collapse of the Han dynasty and the breakdown of many other powerful regimes. In other words, how do we know what constitutes failure, and what evidence do we need? Laments for the good old days written by elites? Fewer imported luxuries found in archaeological sites? Shrinking average sizes of cattle bones, which probably indicates worsening nutrition? Is a declining number of written government documents a sign of anarchy or of less effective repression and exploitation? What do we value more: Conditions that facilitated the maintenance of great buildings and urban theaters that left behind classic plays? Or opportunities for huge numbers of men, women, and children to escape their enslaved status?

A historical approach addresses life's big questions: Who are we and how did we get here? It does so by sowing doubt, but also by looking for systemic patterns in humanity's enormous range of variation. How do we understand evil? Then, and more painfully, how do we make sense of people's willingness to accept or even defend it? Has there always been human slavery and human trafficking? How did we come to view "the nation" as the inevitable context for history, and what happens when we move outside those boundaries? Do all human beings behave essentially the same way? Does invoking context make excuses for evildoers? Are there any universal core values, and is all change progress? What separates us from other species? Is having a past distinctive to humans?

These are important questions, not only because they serve a public purpose—which they surely do—but also because asking them is a way for historians to protect our turf. A key point here is that using history well involves, first of all, explaining how to not use it badly: that good historians avoid cherry-picking examples to show that something has always been that way and avoid asking students to judge people of the past without first building the fullest possible understanding of their context. We need to model an approach that builds to the big questions slowly: through examining a wide range of cases, taking account of multiple perspectives on those cases, and always asking what any interpretation, including our own, says about both the topic and the authors of the interpretation.

Thus, effective teaching requires that we do more than just provide something as close to a true account of the past as possible—as if we were writing on a clean slate. Instead, it demands raising awareness of widespread but often semiconscious beliefs and explaining where they come from, why they are not (or only partially) true, and the consequences of believing them. Think back to the Chinese and American narratives of World War II discussed earlier—it's easy to see how each of those tales might condition citizens to see their nation as capable of relying on itself alone, rather than on allies, and to regard the exercise of its power as a good thing for the world at large. (Other nations, of course, have similar narratives; Russia's has been very much on display of late, mobilized to support its 2022 invasion of Ukraine.)

In recent years, historians have made progress articulating what parts of our skill set are specific to history (or particularly well-taught in history texts and courses) as opposed to simply calling these skills "critical thinking" (which every department teaches in some form). We have arrived in this different place thanks in part to work from cognitive scientists on how people learn, but also thanks to curricular reforms that have emerged from two different places: broad groups of people demanding that everyone's story be reflected in what we teach, and the idea of backward design that puts big ideas and student learning first. Introductory history courses can demonstrate the presence of common sense—or, if you prefer, ideology—and the peculiar power history possesses to free us from its errors. In the classroom, we can interrupt smooth narratives to make the case that historians have expertise to impart above and beyond the facts that students may learn (facts that are often readily available via a quick web search). Challenging common sense and calling attention to our method helps make the case for undertaking a more reflective process than simply elaborating on what we already "know," just as proving that the earth cannot be flat (even though it seems to be) provides an accessible but powerful demonstration of learning to think scientifically.

In the summer 2005 issue of *Daedalus*, educational psychologist Lee Schulman posed the following question: "Is there, or should there be, a consistent connection between the way a discipline creates or discovers new knowledge and the way it apprentices new learners?" This notion comes from the world of educational design, and it serves as a model for teaching and initiating students into the world of professions. At its simplest, the goal is to create pedagogy that reflects what professionals in the field do and the worldview in which they operate. So what do we, as historians, actually do? We question narratives, we make sense of facts by adding contextual caveats or breadth, and we express doubt and ask questions about materials that have survived in various conditions from the past. Thus, design theory suggests, we should organize courses so that they introduce students to precisely these principles and practices. If history has a signature pedagogy, it rests on those rhetorical moves and the continuous skepticism they engender.

Given the potential range of introductory courses, how can instructors begin to help students learn to do this challenging thinking for themselves? And how can we do this by using what students know about their world and what they think they know about the past? Let's start by using Schulman's insights to question familiar tools: the hefty textbook and document collection that offer some coverage and experience in working with primary sources. Textbooks tend to erase doubt, debate, and shifting perspectives and generally hide interpretive moves in favor of providing a smooth narrative and a mountain of ostensibly noncontroversial "background" information; thus, this model provides little evidence of what historians actually do, and may actually obscure it. And while reading primary sources is indeed part of what historians do, it is only one part: most of us spend as much time reading each other's work and debating the interpretations of history therein as we do on original research. This makes it a serious problem to omit secondary readings, which provide good examples of how we figure out the significance of our sources and what materials from the past can be useful sources in the first place. The problems created by such an omission are made worse if this leaves the textbook as a course's sole example of what historical inquiry produces.

What kinds of assignments might make an introductory course into a forum where students see the power of historical analysis, truly introducing them to the discipline? There's no one way to do this, nor one kind of intro course that consistently does it best; suitable techniques will vary across institutions, times, places, and the idiosyncratic strengths of particular students and faculty. The key disciplinary habits that we laid out earlier—introducing analysis and skeptical reading, assessing common knowledge, practicing skeptical reading and taking perspectives, and catalyzing doubt to revise a claim with new evidence—are challenging to name and to teach. But here are some concrete examples we've seen work in our classrooms.

Imagine that your course has, as some of its deepest hopes, for students to stand in someone else's shoes; understand that there are different perspectives about events; feel and express uncertainty. What comes next? Designing assignments that require each of these elements. Let's take Reconstruction, an endlessly debated era in US history. During a presentation or discussion, lay out the conflicting hopes of the formerly enslaved, elite white southerners, poor white southerners, white northern politicians, etc. Then have students work in groups and, after reading documents written by Freedmen's Bureau officials and by white and Black southern newspaper editors, present their answers to the following question: "At the end of Reconstruction, who had achieved more of their goals: the formerly enslaved or their former enslavers?" Then let all the students see what evidence each group has used to support their case, from both lecture and the documents. This could be a one-off exercise or preparation for an essay. None of these skills is natural or self-evident; each contributes to a curriculum that serves a set of goals beyond content knowledge.

Another useful exercise playing on "what everyone knows" involves considering words like "freedom" or "citizenship." Defining those terms in the present is a fraught exercise; asking concrete questions about what they meant in the past—and how much the answers depended on who you were and where you lived—can open a conversation rather than shutting it down. So ask students to explore the question either in discussion or as an essay prompt: "What did citizenship mean to different kinds of people living in the new United States?" You can leave the question wide open or set up some specific cases: a Cherokee leader, a Virginia enslaved mother, a New Orleans painter, a New York printer, a South Carolina preacher. You can push the question further and ask students to demonstrate whether and how these people (individually or as members of communities, overlapping or in conflict) might have benefited from the American Revolution. Your job as the instructor is ensuring that the question of "who benefits" stays open, with lots of possibilities in the air or on the board, allowing students to see how much context and positionality matter as definitions shift.

Another way to create productive doubt is to widen the lens by using social science modeling and comparison as analytical moves that enable us to see both similarities and differences in human behavior across time and space. Models that claim cross-cultural validity tend to rely on universal needs, such as hunger, thereby highlighting similarities rather than differences. And indeed, since all people need food, there is some utility to models that correlate bad harvests to social unrest. But all people also live in societies with cultural values, so no society treats all foods—or sexual partners, to use another biologically driven example—as equally appropriate for all people or on all occasions. Cultures always have rules, and abiding by those rules means that some behavior we might deem irrational makes perfect sense to the people we study. To put it differently, there will always be some elements of what historical actors did that universal models cannot explain and that force us to consider culturally based differences. For example, rioters in western Europe who seized food between the 16th and 18th centuries from those who charged "excessive" prices often left behind what they considered a fair price for what they had taken forcibly, even though they were typically poor and could surely have used that money for other necessities. They did so not because they were forced to, but because they wished to see themselves (and be seen by others) as acting justly rather than as thieves.

Moreover, what it takes to justify a person's actions—to themselves and to their peers—will vary across time and place, though the need for self-justification can itself be found everywhere. Qing tax protestors, for instance, were less inclined than their Euro-American contemporaries to reject outright the government's right to levy particular taxes. But they could react aggressively if local officials seemed to be pocketing illegal surcharges or failed to lower rates during bad harvests (a measure that Europeans did not necessarily expect of their governments). Consequently, though Qing tax protestors sometimes sacked a government compound, they generally left untouched the portion of tax revenues they believed legitimate—much like "just price" riots against European merchants. Walking students through such similarities and differences helps them see how historical comparisons can be used to sort out what is universal (people get angry if they feel exploited, especially during hard times) and what is not (particular understandings of what constitutes exploitation). To take an extreme example: that rioters in Naples threw a shipment of potatoes into the harbor during a famine in the 1760s—calling the tubers "slave food"—amounts to little more than a curiosity if we dismiss the rioters as simply ignorant. If, on the other hand, we ask *why* they considered the potatoes a grave affront to their dignity (while acknowledging that they may well have been at least partially ignorant of the potato's nutritional value), we might achieve a rare glimpse into how people who left behind very little writing thought about their status as free people—precisely because they felt strongly enough about this point to harm their own material interests in the service of asserting it.

Much like a good journal article, then, a single class should include narrative and analysis, a beginning and an end. Asking students to consider a puzzle about an image or a document that raises some doubt or big questions can help them see that there are multiple options but that some explanations simply don't hold up. Take a careful look at a single case study with multiple answers. Then conclude with a raft of questions. Which explanation makes the most sense? Would the outcome be different if X or Y happened, or if someone else recorded or told the story? Could this have happened in the Classical Era or the Middle Ages, in 1828 or 2004? Pamela M. Kiser's integrative processing model suggests that "knowledge, *having been constructed*, gives students a greater command over it as a tangible, concrete, lasting entity which can be retrieved and used."[4] By the same token, an old idea that students have actively participated in pulling apart will be more effectively dismantled than ideas that have simply been contradicted by a new fact handed down from on high.

---

4. For more on Kiser's model, see Kiser, "The Integrative Processing Model: A Framework for Learning in the Field Experience," *Human Service Education: A Journal of the National Organization for Human Service Education* 18, no. 1 (1998): 3–13.

Encouraging students to see how much context is needed to stand in someone else's shoes, even for a class exercise, is only one step. It is also revelatory to help students build a list of mental baggage to jettison and grasp the radically different "common sense" required if they are to convincingly (if imperfectly) think through the choices available to people of another time. The key, as in so much of our pedagogy, lies in helping students to understand context and question their assumptions, rather than leaping into superficial "empathizing" that does more to affirm their expectations than challenge them.

We have laid out historians' particular ways of searching out, comparing, and contextualizing materials. Again, historians need to name what we do and show students how we do it. Slow down. Analyze a single sentence or paragraph together before moving on to the next. For example, suppose you assign the *Requerimiento*: a document written in 1510 by Spanish lawyers and clerics, originally in Latin, then in Spanish, and then in Indigenous languages such as Ta'no or Quechua. It is a single page, but it is a dense legal and religious document, foreign to most students. Tell the story first, and name that process "contextualizing." What was going on in 1510? Then, what were the intentions of the document's authors, and why did Spanish officials "require" that explorers, enslavers, and ship captains read it aloud to Native people? Have students think through that context and what it might have meant to hear a Spanish document read to Indigenous non-Spanish speakers. Read it together, paragraph by paragraph. Which words do the students need to look up? Consider having them read in smaller groups or by using online annotation tools. Finally, they might write a three-sentence summary that they can share or that you can grade. This exercise, which should take about an hour, can be done in a big class or a small one, but it requires guidance: Why are primary sources tricky, and how can students read and decode a dense, difficult document? To demonstrate that you care about this skill, consider having them read a less familiar document as part of every exam.

Secondary sources, or texts written by scholars about the past, model ways to structure arguments and to showcase a historian's use of materials. Historians often write for other historians, which allows them to assume that their readers know certain things already and share certain ideas about what is important and what constitutes a strong argument; thus, even well-written articles are not always immediately accessible to beginning students. Breaking the code for students—showing them how articles and arguments are structured and how language provides clues to where an argument is moving—is a service they can appreciate whatever their major or future profession. Helping students identify rhetorical devices like narrative openings, straw men, or a "shocking" historical fact or anecdote improves their thinking and writing, as does showing them the keys to finding claims and evidence—"some people have argued X, but now that we have seen Y document, we think Z." Using a well-structured essay, pull out a few big claims and point out examples of that language. With the students, make a list of phrases that indicate pieces of an argument; then get the class to dig around and find examples in an assigned article (choose the article carefully, and make your own list in advance to ensure the class won't come up empty-handed). Once they begin to see the article's key points, ask them to consider who or what the author is arguing against, and why that author thinks it's important to establish a particular point about the past. Why should we care? In short, students can use many of the same techniques on these texts that we do on primary sources. Learning to read critically will aid their doing the same with advertisements, investment prospectuses, social media posts, and other attempts at persuasion they encounter outside the classroom.

Teaching them to read closely also helps students to write with purpose, to get something on paper that might be convincing to other people. The rhetorical moves that we use to build claims also acknowledge, often implicitly, the skepticism we expect from readers. Student writing provides important feedback for instructors: not only to address writing problems but also to assess whether students have learned the moves crucial for making provisional claims. We are training students to write for audiences in the world beyond school. Unlike their teachers, future audiences won't be paid to read their words or to assess their personal progress, and such audiences may be more inclined to dissect—or worse yet, dismiss—their efforts rather than to encourage them. Thinking about the need to engage an audience also highlights the importance of making a point that might be controversial, rather than arguing something nobody could dispute. Many students play it safe—especially nonmajors or those lacking academic self-confidence—and try to minimize the risk of "getting it wrong" by saying something that no one could disagree with. (Every experienced teacher has read too many papers with conclusions such as "A and B agree about some things but disagree about others" or "These two events were similar, but not identical.") We do these students no favors if we encourage a caution so extreme that it stymies intellectual growth.

As all this suggests, historians don't aim to construct one perfect story of the past that is true in the same way that plane geometry is true. But the skills we help students acquire have utility and power if the students learn to see and trust them. This isn't just about experts operating in a profession; it's about developing civic practice and shared public values. We are providing students with tools to assess what they see, read, and hear, and to engage in conversations about the provisional conclusions they've drawn. Studying history requires tolerating uncertainty and ambiguity and seeing that different perspectives can yield insights that are always partial but still valuable.

The "still valuable" part is crucial. Many students come to us thinking that there's stuff (mostly in the natural sciences) that is straightforwardly true or false and other stuff (mostly in the humanities and social sciences) that's a matter of opinion. A good intro course can acquaint and acculturate them to the vast space between rock-solid fact and arbitrary personal preference. Since that space between includes most of the world we all navigate, we perform a service not only for our students but for the communities they inhabit when we make it clear that there are standards for evaluating historical claims—and more broadly, claims about the contemporary social and political world—that aren't as hard and fast as those of a geometric proof but are nonetheless a long way from being as arbitrary as the best flavor of ice cream. Some students may arrive in our classrooms doubtful that there is a standard of truth beyond how many people buy something or like it on social media, or how loudly somebody repeats a lie. Others would not explicitly take that position but lend it indirect support by thinking it is pointless or impossible to engage in reasoned debates about social, cultural, or political issues. Demonstrating to them that there are better and worse accounts of social and historical events is itself a vital accomplishment.

Because we respect our students enough to assume they want to distinguish between propaganda—however comforting—and truth, teaching the introductory course is a huge opportunity. We guide and encourage present and future parents, partners, community activists, politicians, writers, and, yes, history teachers to consider the power of evidence and analysis, to build truth that is always provisional and subject to scrutiny and new data.

Wherever our students' futures take them, they will be bombarded by information and stimuli that are usually decontextualized and often overwhelming. They will ask questions to artificial intelligence bots that are generally judged successful if they accurately summarize the current consensus on a topic, but—even at their best—are not designed to deliberately challenge "common sense." Historians have much to offer students setting out across such a landscape. We began this essay insisting that history isn't dead and that our methods are far from irrelevant. Quite the contrary: our signature skepticism offers a way to take back a measure of control over our "information environment." Reflecting on the past and its meanings for the present might be slow work, but it is vital, exciting, and creative work—and democracy cannot survive without it.

Introductory History Courses in 2021: A Snapshot in Time and the Midterm View

Claire Vanderwood and Julia Brookins

What is important about introductory college history courses? How do faculty understand their function in the undergraduate curriculum? We decided to ask the instructional faculty who actually teach these courses at a variety of institutions across the country. Results from the AHA's 2021 History Gateways Survey on Introductory Courses reveal instructors' ambitious and wide-ranging goals for their courses, as well as the resources individual faculty members deploy to achieve them. They also document instructors' mid-pandemic frustrations. Taken together, the more than 800 survey responses show that introductory history courses are comprehensive vehicles for college learning, in which faculty attempt to serve the needs of students, institutions, and our larger society. Given the difficulty of achieving so many goals in a single course, these responses suggest that clearer prioritization among desired outcomes make the requirements for success more transparent to all students.

An undergraduate-level introductory history course can transform "the way [students] see the world and their place in it." Many faculty members find it challenging to teach classes like these, which feature frequently in general education curricula and can involve students with different skill levels, large class sizes, and broad subject matter. The possibilities of leading what are often students' first and only forays into college-level historical study, however, are great. Respondents to the History Gateways Survey recalled that these courses have the power to help students "increase cultural and informational literacy," and "to learn to think historically and to learn the skills of imagination, skepticism, empathy, and humility."

Building on insights and priorities that the History Gateways faculty and advisory committee identified early in their work, AHA staff member Julia Brookins developed a questionnaire for instructors of introductory history courses at the college level and piloted it among History Gateways personnel. One key issue that arose in initial discussions was the burden individual instructors feel of juggling the many purposes of an introductory history course, which often serves as a workhorse for student learning across the general education curriculum. How do history instructors prioritize among so many goals with limited course time? Another cluster of questions emerged about how these courses could fairly address students' varied preparation for college-level writing and reading while maintaining fidelity to disciplinary and institutional standards of rigor.

With help from Stephanie M. Foote of the John N. Gardner Institute for Excellence in Undergraduate Education, the AHA launched the public survey online in July 2021, distributing the link via emails to current and former members as well as on the AHA's social media. Between July and October 2021, we received 840 substantive responses, which exceeded our expectations in both quantity and detail. Respondents went well beyond the minimum required questions, shared why and how they taught their courses, and offered insights into their students' experiences.

These results capture a culture of postsecondary history education in which faculty report considerable freedom around the content and structure of their courses, while describing the persistent difficulties in resolving the many and varied obstacles to student success. Gateway courses represent just one facet of the broad and overdetermined problem that is college completion. These issues are thorny, but our data suggest that course redesign and more collaboration provide some pathways for improvement.

THE SURVEY AND RESPONDENTS

The survey consisted of 28 questions, including 12 that were required. In order to complete the questionnaire, a respondent had to teach one or more of "any lower-division, undergraduate course that is not reserved for history majors/minors. The courses might be offered outside the history department through a general education or core program with an interdisciplinary orientation. They might be offered through high schools for dual credit or concurrent enrollment." Many questions were multiple choice, some prompted respondents to rate or rank different options, and there were several free-response questions and spaces for comments. (The full list of survey questions can be found on the AHA website.)

Those responding to the survey tended to be experienced faculty who taught at four-year colleges and universities. Overall, responses were deep and thoughtful. Nearly 70 percent of respondents taught at a public institution, and 28 percent at a private college or university. Three-quarters primarily taught students at a four-year college or university, 21 percent primarily taught two-year college students, 2.3 percent taught roughly equal numbers of students at more than one type of institution, and 1.6 percent primarily taught students at a high school (e.g., dual-credit or dual-enrollment students). Relative to the 30 percent of undergraduates in the United States who attended community colleges in fall 2021, two-year faculty were significantly underrepresented among respondents. Despite offering valuable detail on instructors' perspectives and approaches to teaching, these results are not perfectly representative of the history instructors that students will encounter at all institutions.[1]

Most responding faculty had been teaching college introductory courses for more than 10 years, with 28.5 percent having 10–19 years' experience and 33.5 percent having more than 20 years' experience. Thirty-eight percent had taught for fewer than 10 years, with around 10 percent being new to the job (0–2 years' experience).

In terms of employment status, nearly two-thirds of survey responses came from tenured (52.5 percent) or tenure-track (14 percent) faculty members. Despite the widespread public image of teaching assistants grading introductory college students, more than three-quarters (76.4 percent) of respondents reported having no teaching assistants.

After ranking a list of purposes introductory history courses serve (see below), survey-takers were asked to rate agreement with a series of statements. Importantly, 94.4 percent of those who responded agreed somewhat or strongly that "I have the freedom

---

1. National Center for Education Statistics, "Undergraduate Enrollment," *Condition of Education*, US Department of Education, Institute of Education Sciences (2023), updated May 2023, accessed September 15, 2023, https://nces.ed.gov/programs/coe/indicator/cha.

I need to design and teach introductory courses in the way that best reflects what is most important for students to learn." Another 2.5 percent neither agreed nor disagreed with the statement, while only 3.1 percent reported that they did not have sufficient autonomy to deliver the course that would be best for students. We should expect, then, that faculty priorities are the main determinants of course priorities in most settings, despite other influences or constraints that shape particular offerings.

Measuring the Purpose and Outcomes of Introductory Courses

Instructors of introductory history courses are eager to set up students for success, no matter the students' majors. Selecting from a ranked list, most respondents reported that the number one purpose of introductory history courses is to develop "skills and dispositions" that can be used across disciplines. A majority of respondents indicated they *often* use class time to teach students to evaluate sources of information as evidence, a skill applicable to all fields. "I have a lot of engineering and pre-med students," wrote one instructor. This teacher's final assignment "utilizes the skills in writing, critical analysis, argument development, and interpretation and use of evidence that they have learned in the class"—skills pertinent to any lab or scientific study.

The question requiring respondents to rank purposes of the introductory history course listed six choices encompassing more than 50 items (Appendix). The History Gateways advisory committee came up with these items in a brainstorming session regarding learning goals. These items were purposes that they as historians and instructors or as other stakeholders—including students, colleagues in other disciplines, institutional administrators, and employers—had wanted students to achieve from these gateway courses. Based on an average of all rankings, respondents tended to see general interdisciplinary skills as the most important outcome (highest score) and deemed recruitment to a specific history program as least important (lowest score)[2]:

- Contributes to the development of skills and dispositions across disciplines (4.2)

---

2. The numbers below represent an average of all ranking scores for each item listed. Items ranked as most important received a score of 6 and items ranked as least important received a score of 1.

- Contributes to the development of skills and dispositions specific to the discipline of history (3.9)
- Introduces and engages students in information literacy (3.8)
- Fosters identity development and awareness of oneself and the world (3.7)
- Conveys content, including for formal compliance and cultural literacy (particular events, people, narratives) (3.2)
- Contributes to recruitment and preparation for history programs (2.3).

Although developing interdisciplinary skills ranked highest by respondents, the relative parity of scores across all six choices points to the many concurrent purposes introductory history courses inherently serve. Even one instructor who ranked the course's most important purpose as to recruit and prepare students for history programs wrote that they describe the purpose of the course to students as "to teach the skills necessary for them to be successful in any career they choose. These skills being: the ability to collect reliable information, to interrogate the information thoroughly, and to present results clearly and concisely." Whether an instructor's top-ranked purpose is to foster self-awareness or convey content, the study of history entails all these ranked choices.

College-level writing and reading skills are a vital component of the interdisciplinary toolkit that these courses can help students to develop. How best to do this for all students emerged as a key question driving History Gateways work, one with strong implications for student success beyond the classroom. Intro courses typically work to build reading and writing skills while covering specific historical content. Without careful attention to course design and assessment practices, however, college instructors can end up merely rating their students based on differences in previous education, rather than teaching and evaluating all students based on learning in the course.

For example, with reading comprehension fundamental to college history classes, many instructors make some attempt to teach reading skills, but it is unclear whether history instructors are meeting student needs in this area. Respondents noted in free-answer responses that their assignments aim to develop students' reading and writing, but a majority (57.9 percent) indicated they only *occasionally* use class time to explicitly teach

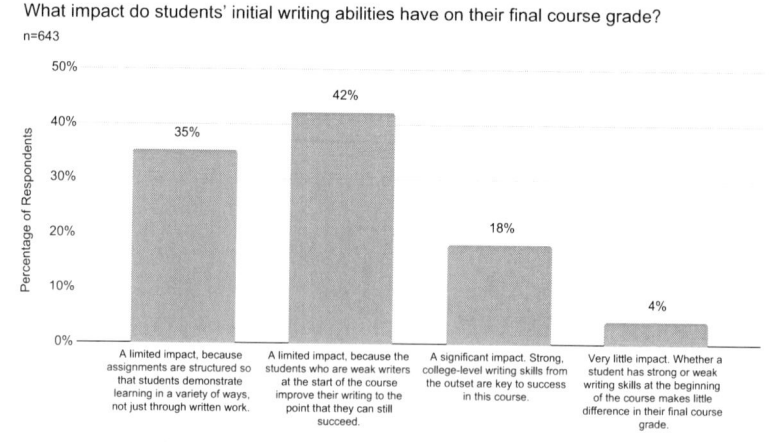

What impact do students' initial writing abilities have on their final course grade?
n=643

- A limited impact, because assignments are structured so that students demonstrate learning in a variety of ways, not just through written work. — 35%
- A limited impact, because the students who are weak writers at the start of the course improve their writing to the point that they can still succeed. — 42%
- A significant impact. Strong, college-level writing skills from the outset are key to success in this course. — 18%
- Very little impact. Whether a student has strong or weak writing skills at the beginning of the course makes little difference in their final course grade. — 4%

What impact do students' initial writing abilities have on their final course grade? (n=643)

Figure 1. Relationship between initial writing abilities and students' final course grades.

students how to improve their reading skills. Most focus on teaching close reading of primary sources—one respondent explained that they use "challenging primary sources as a place to model reading strategies and my analytical method." When it comes to overall reading strategies, though, a lot of instructors discuss them "once early on"—then move on. Some students may need more sustained support.

As for writing, a majority of respondents have designed their course assignments to practice, teach, and assess writing or to reward improvement made during the course (Fig. 1). "Course grading is weighted for improvement," wrote one instructor, "with later essays/exams being worth more points than early ones." Regarding students' initial writing abilities, 41.9 percent of respondents determined that they have a limited impact on their final course grade, as students tend to improve as the course goes on. For 35.6 percent of respondents, initial writing abilities have a limited impact, because students demonstrate learning in a variety of ways, not just through written work.

Still, 18.2 percent of instructors say that strong, college-level writing skills from the outset are key to success in their course. This approach to evaluating student performance presumably serves as an obstacle to less-prepared students and might convey the message that they cannot succeed in college. One instructor put it bluntly: "Sink or swim." While it was a relatively small minority of responses, it still represented a significant number of college history instructors. For those students whose instructors have designed their introductory courses so that final grades are largely based on whether students arrive with good writing skills, the barriers to success in our discipline, and perhaps in college overall, must seem daunting indeed.

Collaboration and Institutional Resources

Our results suggest that most instructors approach course design and teaching as a solo venture. This owes, in part, to limited institutional support. Contrary to public perception, the vast majority of instructors do not work with graduate student teaching assistants; those who do have this support are predominantly tenured faculty members (65 percent). Further, only 30 percent of respondents agreed that they "work collaboratively with faculty colleagues on aspects of the design, teaching, or assessment of our introductory courses." Tenured faculty members, full-time lecturers, and contract instructors were somewhat overrepresented among those reporting that they collaborated, while both tenure-track and part-time faculty were underrepresented among collaborators.

In higher education, at least, history educators appear inclined to work alone. Does it have to be this way? In many contexts, limited resources stretch institutional capacities to their breaking points, but it may be that greater collaboration both within and outside of departments could improve both student learning and faculty well-being.

The growing ranks of academic support staff at many institutions are a case in point. Many campuses, for instance, have writing centers that employ dedicated staff and provide additional resources to help students develop core communication skills. Comparatively few respondents, however, rely on institutional staff and resources for writing instruction. The majority of instructors in every category—graduate students, part-time and contract instructors, and tenure-track professors—do the work of teaching writing skills on their own. The category in which the greatest percentage of people rely on support staff is part-time and contract instructors. Many instructors report that they refer students to the writing center as needed, rather than incorporating the center into the class's structure. One noted that their university discourages requiring all students to visit the writing center, as the center "would not have enough resources to accommodate this." In this situation, more students might benefit from a course design that integrated explicit writing instruction. A well-resourced writing center paired with introductory history courses might do wonders for developing students' historical skill set, but institutional constraints can necessitate other approaches. Whatever the reason, this type of collaboration or regular use of shared institutional resources is not the norm among faculty. The culture of instructional freedom around introductory courses can be a double-edged sword, placing much of the responsibility for student success on individual faculty.

The Promise of Course Redesign

Our survey revealed a number of course design innovations that have allowed instructors to push their students toward a deeper understanding of the world and help them develop a robust historical skill set. These innovations largely had to do with the quantity and quality of assignments, and many were developed in response to the pandemic. In 2021, many instructors doled out less reading than before 2020 or chose to be more selective, with one in particular "favoring depth and opportunities [for] skill-building over diversity and quantity of sources." Many assigned more writing assignments to keep students engaged and provide more opportunities for feedback. "I teach writing in my intro courses very deliberately," wrote one professor. "I use scaffolded writing assignments that layer in more writing skills with each successive assignment: finding primary and secondary evidence, making an argument, structuring the paper and writing a cohesive essay that uses these skills." It seems that offering more scaffolded assignments that build specific skills yielded results for many of our respondents.

Among the other takeaways from the responses was the wide range of course materials that instructors use now in intro courses (Table 1). While two-thirds of respondents still assign textbooks, instructors generally require their students to consider evidence and interpretations in varied formats. The

Table 1. Types of required materials

Source	Number	Percentage
Excerpts of primary sources (outside textbook, any medium)	538	84
Textbook	433	67
Film or video	401	62
Complete primary sources (outside textbook, any medium)	316	49
Online collections of primary sources	302	47
Complete secondary articles or excerpts	293	46
Open educational resources (OER)	216	34
Excerpts of secondary articles or essays	196	30
Artifacts/material culture	192	30
Complete monograph	166	26
Current print or online periodicals/news	150	23
Podcast	131	20
Complete novel	116	18
Other (please specify)	78	12
Social media posts	35	5

highest proportion of respondents, 83.5 percent, required students to use excerpts of primary sources (outside the textbook, in any medium). Textbooks were the next most-required learning material, used by 67.4 percent. Film or video was the third most-required material (62 percent). Other types of sources and readings were cited by a minority of faculty, from complete primary sources (49.2 percent) to social media posts (5.4 percent). How much reading to assign is a perennial question among history faculty, and the limits of student reading skills, time, and attention are likely a significant factor here. How much they can be expected to read structures what faculty assign (Fig. 2). Respondents reported requiring students to read an average of 44 pages in a typical week, with a median of 40. The most anyone reported requiring in a typical week of an introductory course was 100 pages (7.7 percent of all responses), while the least was 0 (a single response).

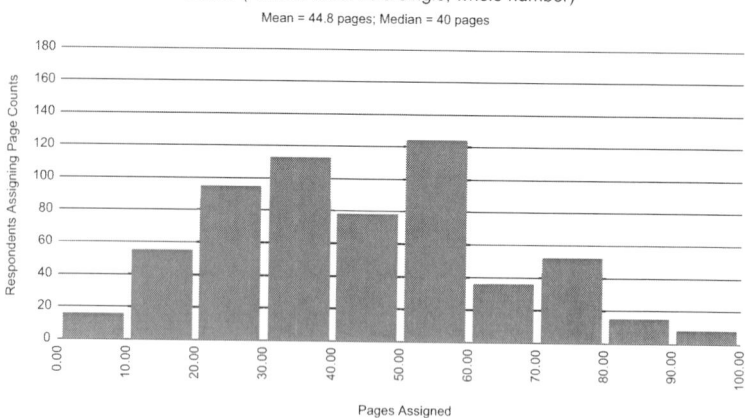

Approximately how many pages of reading do you typically require students to read in a week? (Answer must be a single, whole number)

Mean = 44.8 pages; Median = 40 pages

Figure 2. Pages per week of required reading.

Many instructors were still reckoning with the emergency shift to remote instruction at the time of the survey. Even in the midst of the pandemic, a period of low morale and high administrative disruption, history instructors pressed ahead. The changes they made included posting all their assignments online, employing the flipped model using prerecorded lectures, and holding online tutoring sessions. Multiple respondents became flexible with deadlines and removed late penalties. "We used all of the technology available to teach better," offered one instructor. Some noted that had they more resources, they would change more to make their courses more accessible. "If I had time and support," said one respondent, "I would try to create captioned videos for my online courses of some of the practical lessons I provide in class on topics such as how to search for primary and secondary sources in online databases and archives and libraries, note-taking skills, essay drafting and revisions, citation formatting, close reading analysis, and much more." This comment highlights a tension many instructors feel with their institutions. Though desiring to make changes, one instructor remarked that "it is unclear what my university will allow." Institutional structures and policies may pose roadblocks to course design innovation.

Overwhelmingly, the survey results showed that instructors want teaching to occupy a place of importance in the discipline.

Instructors want opportunities to workshop course design with peers. Instructors want increased resources and professional community around teaching. "I wish there were a LOT more discussion of teaching, in my department and in the discipline as a whole," one respondent shared. "I feel like we all reinvent the wheel over and over again. . . . Imagine if we conducted our research this way!"

The essays and case studies that follow serve as models and prototypes, sketching out approaches that have helped improve student success in a variety of contexts. There is no one single approach that will meet the needs of every institution. But we can continue the time-honored pedagogical tradition of learning from the experiences of others.

While the results of the 2021 survey indicated certain conditions that were specific to the pandemic period, they also offer a clear view of courses at a moment of significant, longer-term transition. History faculty members have more tools and flexibility now than prior to the pandemic, and they are using them to create strong learning experiences for students. The importance of ongoing discussions about course design and pedagogy in the disciplinary community is also clear, and we encourage history instructors to use their professional networks to help them sort through the layers of purposes, needs, and mandates that they must consider in guiding students through the gateways of history learning.

Appendix: Potential Purposes of Introductory History Courses

Historians advising the AHA's History Gateways initiative met in 2019 to discuss the range of goals and learning outcomes that instructors, students, administrators, members of the public, and even lawmakers might have in mind when they think about what a college history course can do. Program staff organized, categorized, and refined the resulting list, sharing it with faculty to help inform their reflection and course design efforts. In the online, public 2021 History Gateways Survey on Introductory Courses, respondents were asked to read through the entire list and rank the six categories of goals from most important to least important, in terms of the introductory course they teach.

Contributes to the development of skills and dispositions across disciplines:
- Help students learn how to be a college student (reading, study skills, understanding instructor expectations, etc.).
- Introduce skills to succeed in college: critical thinking, problem-solving, what to do with course materials; recognizing the relation between one course and other courses.
- Essential concepts and competencies: how to analyze evidence and arguments.
- Teaching students to ask the right questions.
- Learn how to engage in civil discourse (as a practice and a habit).
- Learning information literacy/adult thinking 101.
- Foundational literacy skills, reading and writing.
- Long-term thinking.
- Ability to analyze complex social situations.
- Prepare students for courses elsewhere.
- Workplace competencies.

Contributes to the development of skills and dispositions specific to the discipline of history:
- Connect to existing student interests to the history of anything; show how the past is relevant to what students already care about.
- Pushing against what people think history is, against student expectations; introduction to history as a discipline.
- Previously, the main purpose was to draw students into more history courses; now, the main purpose is to draw students into what historians do. This approach is skills-based: students learn the utility of historical thinking for other majors, too.
- How to think historically.
- Essential concepts and competencies: chronological reasoning.
- Demonstrate the broad range of potentially relevant factors one must consider in order to really understand past events and phenomena; show the need to consider multiple, different registers of human experience together.
- Preparation for historical-mindedness, specifically in careers.

Introduces and engages students in information literacy:
- Introduction to evidence.
- Guide students to understand what kinds of truth they are going to learn during their college experience.

- The heart of an introductory history course is primary sources.
- Students learn to engage carefully with varied sources and evaluate their usefulness as evidence to answer different types of questions.
- Consider a variety of historical sources for credibility, position, perspective, and relevance.
- Students learn to discern sense from nonsense.
- Occupy and give students experience with the terrain between the truth of mathematics and mere opinion. This is specific and useful epistemological terrain with which most are unfamiliar.

Fosters identity development and awareness of oneself and the world:
- Identity: Understanding relationships between the Self and the World.
- Sense of belonging for students—practice in reflection and in self-reflection.
- Where do I (the student) see/place myself?
- Civic identity.
- Make students aware of their own mental, historical narratives, their own biases and assumptions.
- Diversity; encounter with diverse people and pasts.
- Introduce unfamiliar narratives.
- Community and global civic engagement.
- How does the past relate to the present?
- The past is present with us today.

Conveys content, including for formal compliance and cultural literacy (particular events, people, narratives):
- "Survey" coverage of content—provide context.
- State citizenship requirement.
- Teacher training (pre-service).
- Compliance with formal articulation agreements, i.e., two-year college to four-year college transfer.
- Foundational content.
- Cultural and historical literacy.
- If I don't try to teach them X, who will? (To overcome perceived gaps in disciplinary knowledge.)
- Provide a chronological, narrative synthesis of the past as the best way to show students how things are connected to each other.

- Specific content matters because it is how students learn to think from particular evidence toward conclusions.

Contributes to recruitment and preparation for history programs.
- Help students love history.
- Attract majors to history.
- Introduction to the history major.
- Recruit non-majors to take more history courses.

Meeting Diverse Needs

TEACHING REFLECTION

THE UNANTICIPATED REWARDS OF PEDAGOGICAL REFORM

Theresa Case

In spring 2019, a team of historians at the University of Houston–Downtown (UHD) launched the History Gateways project in partnership with the American Historical Association and the John N. Gardner Institute for Excellence in Undergraduate Education.[1] Using the Gardner Institute's Gateways to Completion (G2C) process promised to guide our team in reshaping UHD's core history courses toward boosting student success rates. Like most college instructors, our team members struck a delicate balance between teaching, service, and scholarship. Only a year later, a worldwide pandemic severely tested our ability to keep all those balls in the air. The central question became how to teach effectively and empathetically in a period of profound crisis for our students, their families and loved ones, our friends and relations, the university, and the world. While emergency circumstances sometimes see people turn inward, our UHD team was lucky to have already established connections with the network of scholars associated with G2C well before COVID-19 upended our lives. Rather than withdrawing, the G2C project coaxed me to move beyond my provincial setting at UHD and listen to experts on teaching and learning from across the country. As team leader, I brought basketfuls of ideas back to my colleagues about ways to refine the UHD history program's core courses. With the G2C process, we determined how best to proceed and

---

1. A note of heartfelt appreciation to the Gateways to Completion team at University of Houston–Downtown: Austin Allen, Jonathan Chism, Joseph Davey, Nancy Lopez, Gene Preuss, and Matthew Bunin. Thank you also to David Ryden, who encouraged the team's efforts, and Mik Yegiyan, our data expert. Special recognition goes to Jonathan Chism, who initiated the application for the Texas Higher Education Coordinating Board Completion Grant and led much of the grant's work, which brought successful outcomes for many students.

made significant headway—especially among underrepresented students.

Plodding Along with Blinkers On

Initially, the prospect of improving student performance in introductory history courses seemed out of reach. Though the history faculty had instituted some reforms before G2C that gradually improved ABC rates, we still seemed to be buckling under the weight of certain burdens: the heavy course and workload that students often took on, a disdain for history that many learners acquired in high school, poor study habits, general hardship, and the uncertainties visited on students, faculty, and staff from the hurricanes, tropical storms, and winter emergencies that severely disrupted everyone's ability to carry on. Meanwhile, the busy schedules among history faculty inhibited our capacity to embrace the full range of student success initiatives. Historians at UHD tend to serve on labor-intensive committees and hold to high standards for scholarship. We also carry a heavy teaching commitment; specifically, a three- or four-course load (five for lecturers), enrollment caps of 50 students per core history section, and no teaching assistants or graders. There were other attitudinal barriers from which I was not immune. I assumed, for instance, that a D was acceptable to many students, since a D still earned credit toward a UHD degree. I arrived at this idea in part based on one student's not atypical response to my advice that he strive for a B or C instead of settling for his D: to graduate, he believed, "All I need is a D." I also expected that a student who received an F was likely to return, retake the course, and recover from their earlier missteps. Neither of these assumptions were correct.

Meaningful Yet Circumscribed Reforms

Prior to the G2C project, the UHD history program focused a good deal on the structure of core courses, standardizing certain features of a course across sections. This brought solid improvement in the DFWI rates for history gateway students. One area of common ground was exam windows: similarly timed exams that allow students to access academic support through the Supplemental Instruction program. The instructors of the course US History before 1877 developed a common assignment so that faculty could act more cohesively and deliberately. Another area of common ground—a project called the Signature Assignment—was adopted by the university in line with state requirements. The history program developed templates for this assignment, which allowed the university to assess the extent to which history gateway students could communicate in writing and think critically by the end of term.

Though the introduction of the Signature Assignment forced me to reexamine my priorities and reorient my core classes toward skill building, it did not change the dynamics of my classroom or ask me to examine my teaching from the students' point of view. My conviction was that students should love history; I could not fathom why they would not find the subject inherently riveting. Seeking to show students how much they were missing, I created elaborate slideshows with arresting images—photographs, maps, paintings—and experimented with an array of gripping readings in lieu of a giant textbook. I emblazoned a quotation by historian and educator Sam Wineburg across my syllabi, as if his words would strike students like lightning and power them through the next 15 weeks: "Mature historical knowing teaches us to . . . go beyond our own image, to go beyond our brief life, and to go beyond the fleeting moment in human history into which we have been born. History educates ('leads outward' in Latin) in the deepest sense."[2] Together, these changes generated excitement and openness to history among my students, but they remained top-down in nature, driven by my cynicism about what was possible given our constraints.

Indeed, the hurdles to pedagogical reform loomed large. Because core history courses were capped at 50 students per section, any revision or addition multiplied the number of an instructor's teaching duties while large class sizes hampered robust class discussion. Although the UHD history program regularly pushed for lowered course caps, faculty were told that the financial costs made reduction impossible. All of this suggested to me that there was not much we could do to affect the academic success of core history students, and I feared that a more substantive overhaul of my teaching would send my semester spinning out of control and rob me of any time for research, writing, and

---

2. Sam Wineburg, *Why Learn History (When It's Already on Your Phone)* (Univ. of Chicago Press, 2018), 24.

service. We faced too many restraints, I reasoned; the best way to proceed was to make the effort without disturbing our basic conception of the history gateway courses.

Going "Beyond Our Own Image" of the History Core

The G2C project revitalized my belief that even instructors who labor under considerable restrictions can make a consequential difference in the academic success of students. The national data collected and analyzed by the Gardner Institute persuaded our team of UHD historians that fundamental reform was imperative. Between 2012 and 2015, about one in four college students nationally received a D, F, W, or I in a history gateway course. The main factors shaping success rates were race, social class, gender, and first-generation status. The numbers on retention were also jarring. Students who received a D or an F in a core history class often dropped out of college. I knew that retention was low but had not grasped the correlation between low retention and those D and F grades in history gateway courses.[3] For a significant number of students, in other words, the message behind a poor or failing grade was not "try again," but "you do not belong here." Many students took this message to heart and left.

The G2C process had us broaden our scope and interact with key institutional actors at UHD and experts on teaching and learning at the Gardner Institute, the AHA, and UHD's Center for Teaching and Learning Excellence. Our Gardner Institute faculty advisor, Betsy Griffin, shepherded us through critical points in the three-year process as we moved from the institutional study to recommendations for action, and then to piloting strategies and evaluating outcomes. Engaging with knowledgeable colleagues both within and outside UHD produced innumerable "aha!" moments in which our comprehension of the problems and possibilities facing us clicked into place. These realizations led our team to undertake changes that directly and positively impacted core history students.

Our G2C history team consisted of five full-time faculty and one to two long-time adjunct faculty. The first leg of the project

---

3. See Andrew K. Koch, "Many Thousands Failed: A Wakeup Call to History Educators," in this volume.

involved educating ourselves about our own circumstances. This exercise—which was lengthy, in part because it required an IRB application—acquainted us with UHD's data on ABC rates and the distribution of ABCs according to categories, including race, ethnicity, gender, and full- or part-time status, for all gateway courses. Like many other introductory courses at the university, student success rates for history gateway courses followed the troubling national patterns identified by the Gardner Institute. This component of the project also had our team conduct a self-study, sharing answers and perceptions concerning advising, scheduling, and assessing history gateway courses, as well as information about academic support services, dissemination of data on DFWI rates within the institution, student opportunities for feedback and practice, the degree to which common standards or texts are in place, supplemental instruction, and core faculty members' professional development opportunities in both online and face-to-face instruction.

"Leading Outward"

As chief liaison to the G2C project, I brought our findings and impressions to several university-wide steering committees, which accomplished exactly what G2C designed them to do: they corrected some of our team's mistaken perceptions and gave us much-needed context and advice. These committees consisted of major institutional actors such as the chair of the General Education Committee, our college's assistant dean and head of advising, and the directors of first-year composition, critical race studies, the Center for Latino Studies, the Center for Teaching and Learning Excellence (CTLE), and the Academic Support Center (ASC). From this fruitful collaboration, our team learned, for example, that the Gator Success Center serves all UHD students—not only first-time in college students (FTICs) as many of us had thought. We also took seriously the suggestion that we bear in mind the writing challenges for nonstandard and nonnative English speakers. Specifically, the proposal was to engage students' arguments, ideas, evidence, and reasoning while applying "minimal marking" for errors in grammar, syntax, and punctuation. Another insight from meetings with the steering committees was that students likely stumble most over particular "tripping points" in the course. Identifying the learning goals as well as the assignments that most befuddle students would allow us to design targeted interventions, smoothing the pathway to success.

Finally, our steering committee colleagues suggested we find ways to inspire students to learn about history. This comment landed with me in a way it had not before. The history program faculty had noticed a lack of student motivation, but like many practitioners in their field, I had long nursed a belief that passion for the discipline alone could convince students of history's value. Through a process akin to osmosis, I supposed, exposure to "great works" of history and compelling quotations, images, questions, and narratives would bring most students inexorably around. Thanks to instructor enthusiasm and expertise—as well as the increased cooperation among core history faculty ushered in by standardization—the history core had seen steady improvement in ABC rates over the years. Still, there was no escaping the fact that I had lost, or had never secured, the commitment from many students to find success in my history core classes, and that to march on blithely with the same approach would reproduce rather than transcend social inequalities.

This epiphany could have led the team to despair over our own ineffectuality. We could have proposed martyring ourselves with ambitious plans to overhaul the core in ways that would burn out already hardworking history gateway instructors. We could have shifted the burden of responsibility to those powerful external forces that undermine many students' academic performance. As one Gardner Institute conference presenter remarked, all three were responses that team leaders would feel obliged to hear out before posing the alternative avenue, which is to ask ourselves (I am paraphrasing): "What can we do in *our* classrooms—what can we handle and sustain—to bring constructive change to this situation?" That caution, to take a moderate, constructive approach, persuaded me that the G2C project was both a vital and a practicable endeavor. I began keeping a running log of promising new strategies (a "smorgasbord") categorized according to whether they necessitated changes at the program or the institutional level. I also made a distinction between approaches our team reasonably could implement with the 50-person-per-section enrollment cap and approaches that would have to wait for lowered caps.

With a course release from my department and funding for conference attendance from the university, I embarked on a tour of the scholarship on teaching excellence. After reviewing some basics—on the "un-coverage" model, history and critical thinking, and the science of learning—I seized opportunities to attend Gardner Institute webinars, AHA sessions on teaching, presentations by the leadership of New American History, and workshops sponsored by UHD's CTLE.[4] The CTLE awarded our team two internal grants, called Teaching Circles, that funded stipends for G2C faculty participants and professional development. Over the project's three-year lifespan, I uploaded my notes on these events to our G2C site on UHD's learning management system (LMS)—which all team members could access—and regularly shared revelations gleaned from these materials with the team. The mountains of information may well have overwhelmed the team if not for the interventions of Betsy Griffin, a Gardner Institute vice president and resident scholar who served as our faculty advisor. Griffin was our anchor during the G2C process. I routinely consulted with her about our data collection, our data interpretation, and the best strategies to pursue in light of our institutional self-study findings. She read about our progress with an expert outsider's eye and recommended opportunities and limitations that had escaped me.

SOBER-HEADED, TARGETED, PIVOTAL ACTIONS

In spring 2021, the G2C history team piloted a series of strategies. Though the strategies may appear meager at first glance, the pandemic's spread and our traditionally large teaching responsibilities required that we move slowly. Each team member created a "welcome video" based on a motivational learning course that I had completed on the advice of the CTLE. This video was not a tour of the LMS site or the syllabus but a means to connect with students on the first day of class and stir their intrinsic desire to learn by addressing common questions they might ask themselves about a new course: Can I do this? Do I want to do this? Do I belong here? The welcome video aimed to inculcate a sense of belonging,

---

4. Baseline readings include: Joel Sipress and David Voelker, "The End of the History Survey Course: The Rise and Fall of the Coverage Model," *Journal of American History* 97, no. 4 (March 2011): 1050–66; José Antonio Bowen and C. Edward Watson, *Teaching Naked Techniques: A Practical Guide to Designing Better Classes* (Jossey-Bass, 2017); Sam Wineburg, Joel Breakstone, and Mark Smith, "Do We Know What History Students Learn?," *Inside Higher Ed*, April 3, 2018, https://www.insidehighered.com/views/2018/04/03/historians-need-measure-what-their-students-learn-opinion.

to convey the fact that intelligence is not fixed, and to establish some sense (briefly) of the course's purpose and relevance—all enormously important ingredients of student success in college. We identified exams as a "tripping point" in the history gateway courses, incorporated lessons on "how to answer a prompt" well before the first exam, and added reminder lessons prior to subsequent exams. Finally, we promoted the Writing-Reading Center as a resource for students as they prepared for their essay exams and the Signature Assignment. The center's director generously agreed to produce a 10-minute video tailored specifically to history gateway students. We highlighted this video in our classes, and some of us hosted a class visit by the director to further the goal of giving the center a human face and combating the stigma often attached to tutoring.

Beyond the team's collective interventions, individual team members opted to take on one or more of the following: frequent writing practice, reading quizzes, exam wrappers or reflections, study tips from former students, a "why history?" lesson on the transferable skills that historical study hones, and more class discussion, particularly using the social annotation tool Perusall. All were methods brought back from various CTLE trainings, Gardner Institute webinars, AHA sessions, and professional development courses. For my part, I experimented with my gateway course section by organizing numerous class days around a puzzling artifact (e.g., a photograph, a statistic that contradicts common knowledge, an unfamiliar image) or some bewildering aspect of the past (e.g., Why did ratification of the women's suffrage amendment barely succeed?). I took this idea directly from Anne Hyde, whose AHA presentations persuaded me to share with students the idea that doubt is "at the core of what historians do" as well as methods to "manage doubt."[5] I created short written assignments around the digital tools fashioned by the New American History: American Panorama, BackStory, Bunk, and the Future of America's Past. Armed with this array of videos, digital atlases, podcasts, and curated secondary sources, students

---

5. Anne Hyde, "Plagued by Doubt: Uncertainty as History's Pedagogy," American Historical Association Texas Conference on Introductory History Courses, University of Texas at Austin, September 28, 2018, https://youtu.be/8zDHlq6LjLQ; and Hyde, "Uncertainty, the US Survey, and Reclaiming a 'Required Course,'" 2020 Virtual Texas Conference on Introductory History Courses, September 17, 2020, https://youtu.be/4uS9cQg3J6E.

explored history with their curiosity in the driver's seat, settled on their topic, and wrote about everything from staged locomotive crashes to the 1919 Chicago race riot, the popular 1930s prison football team the Black Sheep, "diving horse" shows, and the utopian Merrymount colony—stories they most likely had never heard before.

The team also committed to implementing a second round of piloted strategies to increase student visits to UHD's advisors and supplemental instructors. This commitment grew out of an observation from a CTLE workshop: students who can be convinced to walk through the door of the Writing-Reading Center will continue to avail themselves of this and other resources. The presenter cited a study that found large improvements in average GPAs for UHD students who received tutoring. G2C history team members decided to offer students the chance to improve a paper grade if they revised their composition with Writing-Reading Center guidance. Members scaffolded the Signature Assignment—breaking it down into segments and providing support along the way—and, along with a non-team core history faculty, hosted two Signature Assignment "bashes" to aid students in interpreting knotty primary sources. The in-person "bashes" attracted between 50 and 60 students; those who could not attend had the option of watching a recording of the event.

From Pilot to Program

Once our team had built up some momentum, we began to spy new avenues for applying the insights drawn from G2C to the UHD history program's gateway courses generally. In fall 2021, the history program adopted, and the university General Education Committee approved, a revised Signature Assignment template that followed the guidelines for Transparency in Learning and Teaching (TILT), a method I became acquainted with through my involvement with G2C and eventually brought into all my undergraduate classes. TILT calls on faculty to provide oral and written instructions that clearly state the assignment's long- and short-term purposes (how it aids the student in meeting learning objectives); step-by-step instructions on the tasks necessary to complete the assignment successfully; and a checklist that delineates the criteria for success. Research indicates that these components positively affect students across the board but resonate especially with underrepresented students.[6] The revised Signature Assignment template included an explanation of the assignment's aim that was designed to appeal to a wide variety of majors, a more fully fleshed-out list of recommended tasks, and a series of examples and clarifications to help students understand the thornier aspects of the prompt.

In the summer of 2021, my colleague Jonathan Chism and I were awarded a completion grant by the Texas Higher Education Coordinating Board (THECB) to enlist broad participation from history faculty in student success initiatives. The grant funded stipends for each strategy that a faculty member trained for and adopted. Participants had the option of choosing to use Perusall for at least two class readings; incorporating a "multipronged" approach (a motivational learning-based welcome video, "how to answer a prompt" lessons, and integration of academic support services video sessions or class visits); and earning a badge for attending a CTLE workshop and applying at least one of its recommended methods. All told, nine core history instructors completed the terms—three adjuncts in addition to five full-time faculty team members—out of 15 full- and part-time history gateway instructors. In fall 2022, the THECB approved extending the grant so that participants could receive training in Perusall's AI grading feature.

ENCOURAGING RESULTS: MANY THOUSANDS RISE?

Happily, our efforts to bolster student success paid off. Between spring 2021 and spring 2022, the history core courses' ABC rates improved by an average of 8 points. These gains were especially pronounced among African American and Asian American students. Black students' share of ABC rates rose 14 points. Asian American students did 9 points better in spring 2022 than the previous spring. Latinos/as made more modest strides—7 points better than one year prior. Moreover, participation in the Student Learning Gains Survey (SLGS)—developed by the Gardner Institute

---

6. Mary-Ann Winkelmes, "The Unwritten Rules of College: Creating Transparent Assignments That Increase History Students' Success Equitably," Brandeis University Center for Teaching and Learning, 2019, https://chep.teaching.vt.edu/content/dam/chep_teaching_vt_edu/2020chep/Winkelmes.pdf; Dan Berrett, "The Unwritten Rules of College," *Chronicle of Higher Education* 62, no. 4 (September 21, 2015), https://www.chronicle.com/article/the-unwritten-rules-of-college/.

and administered in most of the history gateway classes during fall 2019, spring 2021, and spring 2022—was highest in 2019 and 2022. In spring 2022, 31 percent of those enrolled in history core sections completed the SLGS. Sections taught by instructors involved in the G2C or THECB initiatives made the greatest strides (all but one G2C team member participated in the THECB project). The written portion of the survey had students respond to this prompt, among others: "Please comment on how the class activities (discussions, group work, an/or hand-on class activities) helped your learning." The overwhelming majority of comments either agreed that this feature of a college class is important to learning or conveyed that their class exercises on this front were helpful to them. The results indicate that history gateway instructors should continue to engage with students and practice the craft of history as a class, whether online or face-to-face.

These results are heartening. In fact, the future of student success in the UHD history core seems bright. In fall 2022, the course cap per core history section was lowered to 40 students, aiding our ability to focus on student success initiatives. Three G2C team members have participated in a CTLE Teaching Circle dedicated to developing a common service-learning project for our history core classes. Student demand for face-to-face classes has expanded, affording instructors the chance to take full advantage of the possibilities for direct and immediate interactions in the physical classroom and thus to nurture and strengthen those crucial connections between students and professors, among students, and between students and their on-campus resources. Regarding our online classes, our history team now understands much more than we did before COVID-19 about how to design intriguing, lively online forums and activities that support a sense of belonging and cultivate an appreciation for the past. Above all, the G2C partnership has impressed upon me the vital need to understand the scholarship on teaching and learning, the pleasure of gaining insights from educators at UHD and beyond, and the degree to which even small, carefully considered steps can have a constructive influence on student performance in history core classes and the faculty who teach them.

TEACHING REFLECTION

NEURODIVERGENCE AND INVISIBLE DISABILITIES IN THE HISTORY CLASSROOM

Celeste Chamberland and Michael Stelzer Jocks

Over the past three years, our participation in the History Gateways project has galvanized our commitment to student success and equitable access to education by providing vital tools for the development of inclusive curricular design. More specifically, by calling attention to how the steep steps of the academy are built on institutional norms of whiteness, wealth, and ability, History Gateways provided a crucial opportunity to address the urgent challenges faced by first-generation and BIPOC students on college and university campuses. Much work remains to be done in our efforts to dismantle the fundamental disparities that have long characterized higher education, and meaningful change can only be accomplished by adopting a student-centered and intersectional approach that takes into account overlapping and often interdependent forms of discrimination experienced by students—namely racism, sexism, and classism. But to create a truly equitable and inclusive space for learning, we must also develop effective strategies to dismantle the pernicious ableism that converges with other disparities in higher education. Although the History Gateways project was not designed to address the specific needs of students with disabilities, its emphasis on student-centered course design and inclusive curricular change equipped us with effective strategies for combatting ableism in the classroom.

Student-initiated accommodation requests are the primary way for those with diverse abilities to navigate the shoals of higher education, but such measures are woefully inadequate and often serve to exacerbate the stigma and isolation experienced by students with disabilities.[1] This anecdotal essay encapsulates our efforts to acknowledge and address the challenges faced by students with the "invisible" disabilities associated with neurodivergence in introductory history classes. More specifically, we contend that efforts to enhance student success in the academy must place ability at the center of discussions about equity and inclusion in tandem with efforts to address the multitude of intersectional forces and challenges that shape student experiences. Rather than viewing disability as a problem needing to be solved, we regard the diversity of bodies and cognitive abilities as an asset and a different way of working that can be recognized only by combating ableism.

In an era of increased teaching loads and service responsibilities, adapting and modifying existing course requirements can take time, a commodity in undeniably short supply for most instructors. Such efforts are worth the value added, however, if they enable us to foster more inclusive learning environments. As neurodivergence, the potential cognitive impact of long COVID, and other invisible disabilities gain public attention and shape the needs of students in introductory history classes, the benefits of inclusive course design will only increase. Adopting a stance that reinforces kindness, empathy, and acceptance is paramount in our efforts to overcome the academy's persistent ableism. To ensure the success of such efforts, institutions of higher education must provide support that extends beyond meeting the legal requirements for a finite range of student accommodations. Given that most faculty have little to no formal training in meeting the needs of students with disabilities, prioritizing institutional support for inclusive teaching is vital to socially just course design. Above all, it is incumbent on every stakeholder in higher education to ensure that *all students, including those with disabilities*, are invited to participate in discussions about inclusivity. Their input will provide the necessary insight to create equitable spaces of instruction and meet the changing needs of our students.

---

1. See Barbara Hong, "Quantitative Analysis of the Barriers College Students with Disabilities Experience in Higher Education," *Journal of College Student Development* 56, no. 3 (2015): 209–26; and Nicole Brown, "Introduction: Theorising Ableism in Academia," in *Ableism in Academia: Theorising Experiences of Disabilities and Chronic Illnesses in Higher Education*, ed. Nicole Brown and Jennifer Leigh (University College of London Press, 2020), 1–10.

In addition to centering the voices of students in our efforts to enhance classroom inclusivity, the interdisciplinary field of critical disability studies (CDS) and the pedagogical principles of universal design for learning (UDL) have provided us with many practical strategies to enhance learning outcomes for students with diverse abilities. Since its inception in the 1970s, CDS has provided a framework to deconstruct the ableist assumptions, prejudices, and social norms that reinforce stigma and create barriers for people with disabilities. Rather than viewing disability as a medical issue, CDS adopts an activist approach that centers the experiences of people with disabilities to contest ableist allocations of resources. Inspired by similar goals, UDL is a pedagogical framework grounded in cognitive neuroscience and design principles of accessibility. As a set of ideals for teaching and curricular design—first defined by the educational theorists Anne Meyer and David H. Rose in the 1990s—UDL confronts ableist classroom inequities by expanding means of engagement, expression, and representation.[2] Based on the premise that a UDL educational environment benefits students of all abilities, implementing such strategies enables greater opportunity for student engagement and more effective pedagogy for all.

Meeting the needs of students with diverse abilities may seem daunting, but it is eminently achievable with a few relatively simple adjustments to course design and a commitment to pedagogical flexibility. Implementing soft deadlines, developing alternative-format assignments, reframing approaches to class participation, and providing regular opportunities for student feedback as a means of monitoring course pace and accessibility represent a few basic modifications that can make a significant difference for students with disabilities. While these changes may seem to undermine scholarly rigor or student accountability, in our experience the opposite has proven true. None of the modifications we implemented necessitated diluting the intellectual sophistication or academic tenor of existing courses. On the contrary, removing traditional barriers to student success unambiguously improved the quality of student work and engaged greater numbers of students in class discussions. Nor were the changes introduced to our courses groundbreaking pedagogical

---

2. See Anne Meyer, David H. Rose, and David Gordon, *Universal Design for Learning: Theory and Practice* (CAST Publishing, 2014).

innovations; indeed, many of our colleagues at a variety of institutions are currently implementing similar strategies. It is our hope that fostering a conversation that acknowledges and addresses the needs of students with disabilities will empower others to recognize the value of classroom inclusivity. Overcoming the force of tradition within the academy—which has historically emphasized inflexible expectations, rigid deadlines, and a one-size-fits-all approach to teaching—remains one of the greatest obstacles in reconfiguring course design.

Based on anecdotal observations of our classroom experiences during the History Gateways project, our reflections are not intended to serve as a comprehensive analysis or data-driven study of neurodivergence and disability; nor are they rooted in specialist knowledge of cognitive science or UDL. Rather, our reflections are intended to think with larger, more formal conversations about the need to address disability in our efforts to enhance equity and inclusion in the history classroom. Disability studies scholars John Horton and Faith Tucker contend that the "daily structures of normalcy" within the academy reinforce an ethos of productivity, performance, and competition that is embedded within the fundamental structures of higher education.[3] Exacerbated by a culture of overwork rooted in neoliberalism, ableist norms of productivity have reinforced a lack of understanding toward those with different abilities both in higher education and society at large.[4] These patterns are particularly pronounced at institutions of higher learning, which prize cerebral dexterity and spurn difficulties in cognition. For neurodivergent students who do not appear to have a disability, this emphasis on productivity and cognitive acuity typically takes the form of inflexible expectations and rigid deadlines that fail to account for the fluctuations in health, energy, or concentration that many students with invisible disabilities experience.[5]

---

3. John Horton and Faith Tucker, "Disabilities in Academic Workplaces: Experiences of Human and Physical Geographers," *Transactions of the Institute of British Geographers* 39, no. 1 (2014): 76–89, here 77.

4. Bronwyn Davies and Peter Bansel, "The Time of Their Lives? Academic Workers in Neoliberal Time(s)," *Health Sociology Review* 14, no. 1 (2005): 47–58; cf. Carla Finesilver, Jennifer Leigh, and Nicole Brown, "Invisible Disability, Unacknowledged Diversity," in Brown and Leigh, *Ableism in Academia*, 143–60, here 154.

5. Finesilver, Leigh, and Brown, "Invisible Disability, Unacknowledged Diversity," 148–49.

First coined by Australian sociologist Judy Singer in the late 1990s, the term *neurodiversity* refers to variations in cognitive functioning associated with a range of conditions, including but not limited to attention deficit/hyperactivity disorder (ADHD), autism spectrum disorders, dyspraxia, obsessive-compulsive disorder, synesthesia, and generalized anxiety disorder.[6] Some chronic illnesses such as lupus, multiple sclerosis, traumatic brain injury, and fibromyalgia may also cause fatigue and cognitive dysfunction that pose ability-related challenges for students in educational settings. Potential obstacles faced by neurodivergent and chronically ill students in the traditional classroom include time-management difficulties, fatigue, problems with concentration and focus, impulsivity, anxiety about speaking in class, and procrastination issues. Since the traditional history classroom is designed for "neurotypical" students, meeting the needs of neurodivergent learners is typically addressed through a finite range of accommodations—such as extended time on tests and assignments—that place neurodivergent students at a disadvantage and contribute to the social stigma they experience by marking hidden barriers as "problems" or leading instructors to underestimate their abilities.

The number of students who have historically requested disability-related accommodations on college campuses may seem small, but it is virtually impossible to determine the actual number of students with invisible disabilities who choose not to disclose their condition or request accommodations.[7] As evidenced by a recent recommendation from the US Preventive Services Task Force that all adults under age 65 receive routine anxiety screening, it seems plausible that anxiety-related diagnoses will continue to increase, as will the number of those affected

---

6. Judy Singer, *NeuroDiversity: The Birth of an Idea* (self-pub, 2017).

7. The National Center for Education Statistics states that in 2015–16, 19.4 percent of undergraduate students reported having disabilities defined by one or more of the following conditions: blindness or visual impairment that cannot be corrected by wearing glasses; hearing impairment (e.g., deaf or hard of hearing); orthopedic or mobility impairment; speech or language impairment; learning, mental, emotional, or psychiatric condition (e.g., serious learning disability, depression, ADD, or ADHD); or other health impairment or problem. National Center for Education Statistics, "Fast Facts: Students with Disabilities," US Department of Education, Institute of Education Sciences (2023), https://nces.ed.gov/fastfacts/display.asp?id=60

by the brain fog and fatigue of long COVID, requiring course design that takes into account fluctuations in cognitive ability.[8] Not only has the experience of living through a disorienting pandemic brought mental health to the forefront, but as Shelley Lynn Tremain, a scholar of biopolitical philosophy, asserts, COVID-19 has also "thrown into relief social, economic, national, racial, and other disparities, as well as exacerbated them."[9] Nearly one-fifth of the North American population will be disabled at some point, making it essential that inclusive course design take into account the needs of students with disabilities.[10]

UDL-inspired modifications also provide a vital tool in efforts to address the intersection of racism and ableism. As evidenced by the work of Kat J. Stephens, a graduate student who has chronicled her experiences as a Black woman with ADHD, Black and Brown students are less likely to receive official diagnoses of their disabilities and are thus often forced to develop strategies of overcompensation or else risk being "written off as having inherently low IQs or being unteachable."[11] Deep-rooted systemic inequities extend well beyond the walls of the academy, but as Kris de Welde contends, "institutional cultures operate to reproduce bias."[12] Although many institutions have sought to rectify such inequities by creating diversity, equity, and inclusion task forces,

---

8. US Preventative Services Task Force, "Anxiety Disorders in Adults: Screening," June 20, 2023, https://www.uspreventiveservicestaskforce.org/uspstf/recommendation/anxiety-adults-screening.

9. Shelly Lynn Tremain, "Introduction: Philosophies of Disability and the Global Pandemic," *International Journal of Critical Disability Studies*, 4, no. 1 (June 2021): 6–9, here 8.

10. Jay Timothy Dolmage, *Academic Ableism: Disability and Higher Education* (University of Michigan Press, 2017), 62.

11. See Kat J. Stephens, "Just a Unicorn," *Journal Committed to Social Change on Race and Ethnicity* 6, no. 1 (2020): 212–16; Sara Ahmed. *On Being Included: Racism and Diversity in Institutional Life* (Duke University Press, 2012); and Lissa D. Ramirez-Stapleton, Lisette E. Torres, Anna Acha, and Ashlee McHenry, "Disability Justice, Race, and Education," *Journal Committed to Social Change on Race and Ethnicity* 6, no. 1 (2020): 28–39. According to Dan Goodley, Rebecca Lawthom, Kirsty Liddiard, and Katherine Runswick-Cole, "much of what passes as Disability Studies implicitly assumes whiteness and risks white-washing the phenomenon of disabled people." Goodley, Lawthorn, Liddiard, and Runswick-Cole, "Key Concerns for Critical Disability Studies," *International Journal of Disability and Social Justice* 1, no. 1 (November 2021): 27–49, here 37.

12. Kris de Welde, "Moving the Needle on Equity and Inclusion," *Humboldt Journal of Social Relations*, no. 39 (2017): 192–211, here 198.

more will need to be done to accomplish meaningful change. It is incumbent on the instructors who serve as the primary point of contact with students on college campuses to address and work toward eliminating implicit biases.[13] Creating more inclusive and equitable course design will not only help dismantle the barriers faced by marginalized students, but will empower all students to challenge binary ways of thinking about identity and ability.

Jay Timothy Dolmage regards invisible disabilities as particularly fraught on college campuses, since students with disabilities are "already routinely and systematically constructed as faking it, jumping a queue, or asking for an advantage."[14] Given the stigma associated with disability, some students may be reluctant to request accommodations.[15] As Jonathan Flowers maintains, "the request for an accommodation construed as an account of the disabled person's existence in the world, becomes a demand for inclusion into the space of the institution . . . while simultaneously transforming the disabled person into a problem for the institution or the organization."[16] Providing accommodation services enables institutions to comply with legal requirements and maintain the appearance of accessibility while reinforcing the normative ableism of the classroom by marking differently abled students as "other." A more pedagogically inclusive strategy would focus on eliminating the need for accommodations entirely by applying the principles of UDL—equitable and flexible use—while providing modes of learning that can be understood

---

13. We are grateful for the opportunities afforded to us through our participation in the History Gateways project and our partnership with the Gardner Institute. Both entities have played a significant role in reinvigorating our approach to teaching by providing access to many evidence-based resources for socially just postsecondary course design. See "Teaching and Learning Academy," Gardiner Institute, accessed May 15, 2024, https://www.jngi.org/teaching-and-learning-academy/.

14. Dolmage, *Academic Ableism*, 120.

15. This is especially true for students with autism spectrum disorders, who report feeling uncomfortable "approaching instructors with any kind of request for support or accommodations because of their fear of retaliation." TC Waisman and Marlon Simmons, "Autism Spectrum Disorder and the Implications for Higher Education," *Journal of Educational Thought* 51, no. 3 (2018): 317–38, here 323; cf. Hong, "Quantitative Analysis of the Barriers College Students with Disabilities Experience in Higher Education."

16. Jonathan Flowers, "COVID-19 and the Disinheritance of an Ableist World," *International Journal of Critical Disability Studies* 4, no. 1 (2021): 107–26, here 123–24.

and deployed regardless of student language skills, experience, or ability to concentrate.

To ensure that students' needs are met, it is essential to include them in conversations about course design. All too often, decisions about classroom layout are made without any input from the very students they are meant to assist; as Dolmage suggests, we cannot fully understand our students' experience of "academia until we interrogate it from the viewpoint of disability."[17] Since few instructors (ourselves included) have received formal training in disability studies, initiating such conversations may seem daunting. But the evidence-based resources of the Gardner Institute—in tandem with recommendations from activist groups such as RespectAbility, ADAPT, and the NeuroDiversity Movement—provide an excellent point of departure for incorporating student voices into meaningful conversations about ability and inclusion in the classroom.

Perhaps the most valuable message we gleaned from our participation in the History Gateways project is the importance of meeting students where they are rather than making assumptions about where we think they should be. A learner-centered approach that takes each student's unique assets and challenges into account is vital to meeting the needs of an increasingly diverse student body. And because student needs are rarely static, equitable and inclusive course design requires consistent monitoring and adjustment. As many of our History Gateways colleagues have underscored, regular opportunities for student feedback and self-assessment through ungraded low-stakes assignments, like exam wrappers and minute papers, remain especially useful in gauging the effectiveness of instructional pace and student engagement.

Exam wrappers—short handouts distributed to students after their graded exam has been returned—provide them an opportunity to identify strengths and weaknesses, reconsider their exam preparation strategies, and reflect on their performance, with the ultimate goal of enhancing future learning. Similarly, minute papers—short in-class writing prompts at the end of class sessions—enable students to identify what they learned in class that day and what remains unclear. These low-stakes assignments

---

17. Dolmage, *Academic Ableism*, 45.

allow students and their instructors to work together in shaping a dynamic learning experience that can adapt to changing student needs.

In our experience, eliciting student feedback through anonymous self-reflection surveys administered several times over the course of a semester encourages students to identify which components of the course are working for them and which are not. Surveys also provide an opportunity to communicate their needs without fear of reprisal or ridicule. When we began administering anonymous self-reflections in our introductory world history classes as a component of our participation in the History Gateways project, we realized that many students who did not feel comfortable requesting formal accommodations felt empowered to disclose how their disabilities have shaped their experiences in the context of an anonymous survey. The results were both illuminating and unexpected. For example, each semester several students with disabilities have indicated that permitting them to doodle in class enables them to concentrate and retain information, a practice we now regularly encourage. Other students have consistently indicated that fatigue and concentration issues interfere with their ability to adhere to rigid deadlines. As a means of eliminating the stressful burden of inflexible due dates, we began implementing soft deadlines, which are recommended but not required. Rather than shirking their responsibilities, the majority of our students continued to submit work on or near the recommended deadlines. Moreover, in the absence of the anxiety engendered by inflexible expectations, the quality of student work—particularly with regard to critical thinking and communication skills—improved noticeably, as did student engagement overall.

In addition to creating opportunities for students to reflect on their learning needs, fostering student engagement through informed discussion remains a fundamental building block of the college experience. However, for some neurodivergent and chronically ill students, responding in the moment without time to mull over ideas before speaking up—especially when called on by name in class—can be counterproductive. This type of "intense social station," as Dolmage terms it, may pose significant difficulties for students who fear they will get something wrong or for those who require additional time to think through their responses. Rather than "using discussion as an informal and camouflaged form of testing," alternative pathways to participation enable students to "do more and better thinking if given more time and different ways to contribute." And "isn't that what we want," Dolmage asks, "more and better thinking?"[18] Rather than imposing a one-size-fits-all approach to student participation, the alternative strategies with which we've successfully met the needs of students with disabilities include providing real-time online learning platform discussion boards for posting comments or questions relevant to class discussion. Online polling services and game-based learning platforms, which enable students to answer questions anonymously through their mobile phones and display the results live, can be a particularly effective means of stimulating class discussion.[19] Over the course of the semester, we also regularly provide blank note cards on which students can submit relevant comments or questions before, during, or after class in lieu of raising their hand or speaking up during discussion.

Alternative format assignments informed by UDL principles can inspire students of all cognitive abilities to meet learning goals. If our aim is for students to understand difficult concepts, "there should be multiple avenues to get to that understanding and to convey it. There should be multiple ways to open that door even if they are redundant."[20] To deploy this strategy in our world history survey, we modified an existing written assignment to include a variety of pathways for meeting two distinct learning goals: to analyze primary sources, and to understand the continuing relevance of ancient history. In one iteration of this assignment, students receive a menu of prompts, some of which take the form of traditional essay questions such as "What was the purpose of the law as envisioned in Hammurabi's Code?" Other prompts provide a less linear route to reaching the assignment's goals, such as creating a fictional dialogue between Hammurabi and a modern political leader about law and justice. Alternatively, students may choose a high-profile legal case

---

18. Dolmage, *Academic Ableism*, 120.
19. For example, our students have responded favorably to Poll Everywhere (polleverywhere.com) and Kahoot! (kahoot.com), both of which offer a variety of free services for classroom use.
20. Dolmage, *Academic Ableism*, 120.

Figure 1. Sahian del Valle, "The Death of Alfred Meyer," 2022. Used with permission of the artist.

and adjudicate it through the lens of Hammurabi's Code by submitting a written response, a recorded presentation, or a short podcast in lieu of an essay.

Although our attempts to create more inclusive and equitable pathways to learning have centered on developing flexible and adaptable assignments, student voices have provided the greatest source of inspiration for our work. Perhaps the most serendipitous moment we experienced during our participation in the History Gateways project resulted from a student's misunderstanding of an assignment's guidelines. The original assignment called for students to submit a brief biographical sketch of one of the men who attended the infamous Wannsee Conference of 1942, in which the SS divulged the Final Solution to mid-level governmental functionaries. In lieu of narrative sketches, and much to our surprise, several students submitted drawings or comics that told a story of the attendees' lives. Our students had taken "sketch" to mean the literal term for drawing, not a narrative overview. After our initial consternation faded, we recognized the pedagogical merits of our "mistake," and we now welcome drawings for this assignment if students prefer. One particularly insightful submission took the form of a painting that depicts the death of Alfred Meyer, who died by suicide next to the Weser River in early spring 1945 (Fig. 1). Although the student had no formal arts training, this powerful sketch captured the spirit of the assignment and effectively conveyed the emotional impact of the Wannsee Conference's dark legacy. Though the submission did not conform to the traditional model of a written assignment, the student had conducted original research, developed a substantive understanding of Meyer's role in the Wannsee Conference, and interpreted the aftereffects of his participation there. If our objective is to empower students to hone their critical thinking skills, analyze the significance of historical events, and effectively communicate an argument, then we should be receptive to the many possible ways of accomplishing that goal.

In *The Decoding the Disciplines Paradigm*, David Pace suggests that traditional approaches to academic instruction risk stifling student creativity by virtue of their rigid emphasis on content rather than the mental operations by which students process information.[21] Rather than enforcing a rigid model of learning outcomes that fails to account for differences in learning style and cognitive abilities, evidence-based educational practices inspired by UDL allow us to anticipate and plan for the needs of all learners. Low-stakes assignments, alternative-format coursework, receptiveness to student voices, and self-reflection surveys represent just a few examples of the many possibilities for inclusive curricular design in the history classroom. Channeling student energies and adjusting to their learning needs can provide a pathway to inclusive course design, dismantle barriers to access, and benefit students of all abilities, backgrounds, and needs.

---

21. David Pace, *The Decoding the Disciplines Paradigm: Seven Steps to Increased Student Learning* (Indiana University Press, 2017), 54–61, 140–42.

CASE STUDY

INTRODUCING HISTORY: ADDRESSING STUDENT BOTTLENECKS WHILE SUPPORTING EQUITABLE AND INCLUSIVE LEARNING

Jennifer Hart and David Pace

ABSTRACT

Driven by faculty concerns about student success in achieving learning outcomes throughout the semester, this project at Wayne State University used the method known as "decoding the disciplines" to identify bottlenecks in student learning and inform the redevelopment of a long-established course.[1] The new course, HIS 1001: Introduction to History, would form the foundation of a more inclusive and equitable departmental curriculum to support learning for a diverse student body. In identifying and addressing bottlenecks to student learning through the decoding process, the project embraced the syllabus as a teaching and pedagogical tool. The assessment of the course redesign pilot highlighted both successes and opportunities for continued development.

CHALLENGE

Serving a highly diverse student body, the faculty of the Department of History at Wayne State University were concerned with two central questions. First, how can we more effectively engage students in the study of history in order to increase the number of course enrollments and majors/minors? And second, how

---

1. Jennifer Hart and David Pace served as project leaders. Other faculty participants include department chair Elizabeth Faue, Eric Ash, Tracy Neumann, Kidada E. Williams, Howard N. Lupovitch, Karen Marrero, Liette Gidlow, John J. Bukowczyk, Hans Hummer, Marc W. Kruman, Janine Lanza, Elizabeth Lublin, William Lynch, Aaron Retish, Sylvia Taschka, Andrew I. Port, and Jorge L. Chinea.

can we help students make steady progress toward their degree while supporting students with wide-ranging educational backgrounds? By rethinking what an Intro to History course might look like, department leadership hoped to address these challenges, which are simultaneous and interconnected. Introductory (1000-level) survey courses constitute a majority of the department's general education course offerings and are also required courses for majors and minors. Reconsidering how we introduce students to history could enhance the development of historical thinking among the general student population (possibly recruiting more students into the major) while laying a solid foundation for history majors and minors to progress steadily through their degree.

Previously, the department undertook regular assessments of student majors and minors by reviewing papers submitted to both an intermediate methods course and a capstone course. These assessments focused primarily on the mechanics of writing rather than the skills of historical thinking. Faculty were increasingly concerned that students were not grasping some of the key methods of historical research and writing in the early stages of their education, leading to weaker performance in upper-level courses. However, in the absence of robust assessment data, faculty struggled to move beyond the anecdotal evidence of their own courses to more systematic pedagogical and curricular reform. Furthermore, and in light of declining enrollments, the department was interested in thinking about how to recruit new students into the major.

In designing a new Intro to History (HIS 1001) course, project leaders worked with faculty to create a pedagogical framework through which to engage students in the development of historical thinking skills. They sought a course that could meet the needs of general education students, provide a strong conceptual foundation for majors and minors regardless of educational background, and attract new students through a thematic focus on timely subjects. HIS 1001 would be designed to serve as a template that could be adapted for other introductory courses and stand as the first in a series, enabling faculty to track the learning development of history majors and minors across their time in the program. By reframing the discussion around historical thinking skills—in contrast to the memorization of facts and dates or the mechanics of writing—HIS 1001 would refocus the department's assessment efforts around the transformation of students from consumers of history to producers of history through intentional and explicit curricular and pedagogical interventions.

Method

The project team held a full day of workshops during which department faculty learned about the "decoding the disciplines" process and applied the method to their own courses to clarify where they saw consistent bottlenecks among majors. In thinking about majors, we simultaneously focused faculty attention on essential historical thinking skills that could be applied to a broader student population at the introductory level. To set the foundation for our discussion and identify common experiences and assumptions among faculty, the conversation began with some general reflections on the skills of history majors and minors. We then applied decoding tools across the curriculum, focusing specifically on two required courses: the intermediate method course, Historian's Craft, and the culminating research capstone course. Looking at recent assessment data and sample student assignments, we walked through each course, identifying the bottlenecks to student learning that frequently show up as gaps between faculty expectation and student performance. We then worked together to create targets for each course level, working backward to move toward the new introductory course. We asked whether we expected students to do X in the capstone course, what knowledge that assumed, and at what point in the curriculum we should guarantee that it be taught.

In shifting conversations from "what do students not know" to "how can we support student learning," the project team began creating a syllabus that could make our discussions concrete and serve as a teaching tool to support inclusive and equitable learning. Such a syllabus would not only provide a map or guide for the course; it would also be a pedagogical tool that modeled the work of historical thinking even as it guided students in their own development.

Outcomes

These decoding discussions highlighted a number of issues. First, faculty were operating on the assumption of basic knowledge that students did not, in fact, possess. The lack of that basic knowledge—What do historians do and how do they do it? What does "historical thinking" mean?—made it difficult for students to master more complicated tasks associated with historical research and writing. In other words, students were often "stuck" in the consumer phase: they received information but did not know how that information was produced or how they might develop the skills to produce scholarship of their own. Second, these skills often constituted a sort of "hidden transcript" of historical knowledge production. The students who came to college-level courses with previous training, beneficial backgrounds, or simply an aptitude for this kind of work were able to navigate the difficult blend of storytelling and analysis that lies at the heart of historical research. But for many students, these skills remained mysterious. Faculty explained that they taught skills like thinking through cause and effect, contingency, and change over time, but they often struggled to point to specific examples in syllabi (either in course content or in student assignments). In other words, faculty often implicitly demonstrated these concepts rather than explicitly teaching students to identify, understand, and apply them as skills.

In response to these discussions, a small group of invested faculty worked together to identify key learning outcomes, and the project leaders developed a syllabus that could not only provide structure for the course but also serve as a pedagogical tool, supporting both instruction and student learning. The skeleton syllabus provided general suggestions for exercises based on best practices drawn from the broader community of historian scholar-teachers. Instructors were encouraged to adapt the structure for their own courses, substituting readings, examples, and some part of the structure or assignments to better fit the realities of their field and subject matter. Learning outcomes connected directly to assignments that assessed student learning in each area: Sources of Knowledge, Continuity and Change, Narrative, Primary Source Analysis, Periodization, and History in Public.

In her capacity as project leader, Jennifer Hart developed a number of infographics to communicate key concepts and serve as reference materials for students (Figs. 1–3).[2] They served as

---

2. Figs. 2 and 3 are also available on Hart's website: https://ghanaonthego.com/2020/08/17/history-methods/.

In this course, you will develop the following historical thinking skills, which are relevant to many aspects of your academic, personal, and professional life:

- Explain the difference between primary and secondary sources
- Identify historical arguments
- Formulate historical questions
- Identify historical evidence
- Analyze primary sources
- Apply strategic reading skills to secondary sources
- Demonstrate change over time
- Examine arguments from different cultural and historical perspectives
- Discuss the politics of knowledge production in history

Figure 1. Learning outcomes from Jennifer Hart's HIS 1001 syllabus.

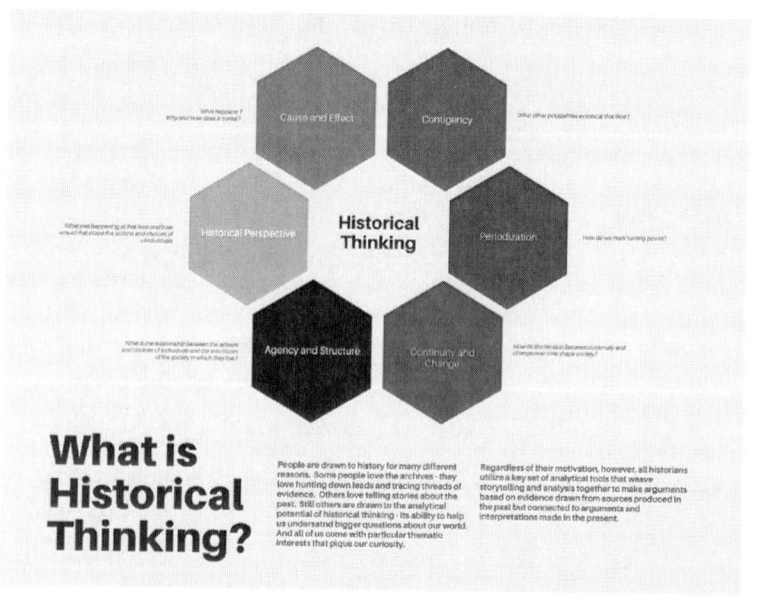

Figure 2. Infographic addressing historical thinking skills to be used as a resource in HIS 1001 courses, designed by Jennifer Hart.

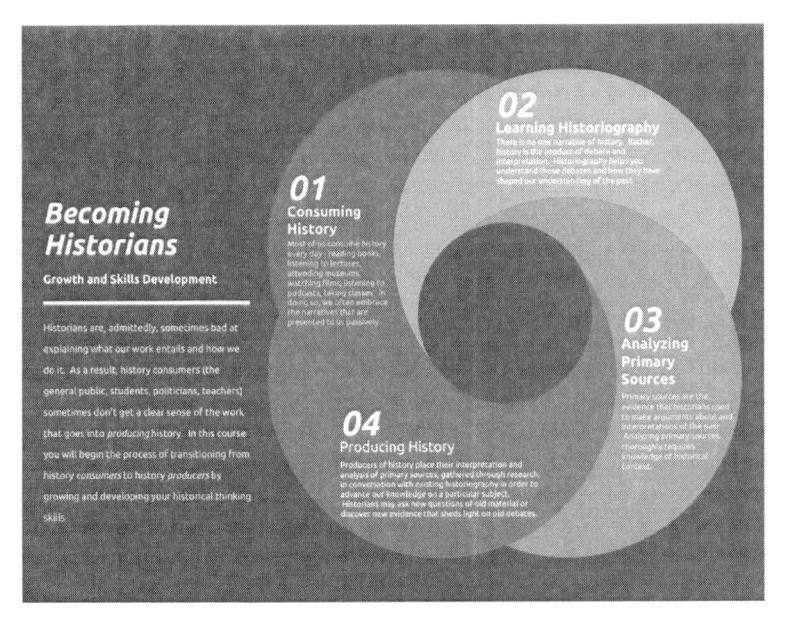

Figure 3. Infographic addressing skills development to be used in HIS 1001 course, designed by Jennifer Hart.

helpful pedagogical tools, keeping instructors and students focused while linking key concepts, syllabi, and assignments to one another.

Impact

In fall 2019, the department approved the course and accepted it as a course of record. Though the course is now listed in the undergraduate bulletin, the department continues to debate the status of the course in relation to the major or minor. This delay highlights two issues to consider when undertaking course development or curricular reform. First, it is important to be realistic about departmental culture while embracing the possibility for growth through targeted faculty development. Second, consistent commitment from departmental leadership, coalition building, and clear and consistent messaging about goals and processes are critical for the successful implementation of these kinds of reforms across the curriculum.

The course was developed in a way that anticipated its adaptation and adjustment in response to faculty needs. Hart continues to experiment with various assignments and structures drawn from the skeleton course, which has enabled her to address faculty concerns about what adaptation might require in their courses and what key elements allow a course to be classed as HIS 1001.

However, this project also points to some ineffable but important consequences of this kind of reform. Regardless of its success, the process generated new kinds of reflection and conversation among colleagues that had ripple effects throughout their courses. Both project leaders embraced external opportunities to share and be in community with other scholar-teachers dedicated to thinking through questions about skills development in historical thinking. They worked through the International Society for the Scholarship of Teaching and Learning in History and the AHA to organize Intro to History workshops that placed their syllabus and strategy in conversation with others. Curricular reform and course development, in other words, are neither local matters nor an end product, but an ongoing process of reflection and adjustment shaped by both the opportunities and limitations of institutions.

This project highlights some possibilities of what departments *could* do and challenges us to think about what we can learn from curricular reconstruction as a form of praxis. Changing norms and structures might be challenging for any number of political, institutional, and cultural reasons—after all, pedagogy is *always* political—but engaging in these kinds of projects can provoke colleagues to think about what they do individually and collectively and serve as a model or lesson for departments operating in other contexts. It is important, in other words, to think about "impact," broadly defined: for the discipline and across the higher education landscape.

The definition of success for this particular project was initially twofold: the implementation of a new curricular and assessment model rooted in HIS 1001, and an improvement in student learning as demonstrated through assessment indicators. However, in negotiating some of the institutional politics related to the project, the definition of success shifted. HIS 1001 became a way to focus faculty energy and attention on articulating their vision for student success in the history department and how they might contribute to that vision in their own courses and across the curriculum.

Lessons Learned

As the project leader, Hart experimented with this structure and many of the assignments in an intro-level survey course in African history during fall 2019 and fall 2020. While the constraints of a survey (as opposed to a thematic course, as HIS 1001 was originally envisioned) made it difficult to adopt the entirety of the HIS 1001 structure, Hart embraced the assignments and course exercises in order to support student learning through the explicit development of conceptual knowledge and skills application. Because the course fulfills a general education requirement in Social Inquiry and Global Learning, the vast majority of students were not history majors or minors, making them ideal candidates for thinking about the relative merit of this model for developing students' historical thinking skills.

By focusing on the analysis of primary sources and the application of historical thinking skills in both classroom exercises and assignments, Hart found that students were better able to understand and articulate what it meant to *do* history. For example, students were asked to complete the sentence "History is . . . " as part of summative and formative assessments. Students who began the course defining history as "events that happened in the past" ended the course with more complex understandings: history as "debates among scholars about what happened in the past based on primary source evidence," "interpretations of the past that weigh different perspectives on events and experiences," and "choices that individuals in the past made and the impact of those choices on themselves and their society." While these are incomplete definitions in various ways, they mark a significant evolution in the sophistication of students' understanding of the work of history and historians. In completing a project that required them to interpret historical research for a public audience at the end of the semester, students were able to consider how they might apply these skills in relevant ways for their own lives and their communities.

Assessment data collected as part of the General Education program provides concrete data points to augment these anecdotal observations. The data highlight ongoing challenges that require reflection and adjustment. In particular, assessment data from the fall 2019 course showed that students were able to describe and analyze historical events at notably higher

Table 1. Summary of assessment results for each learning outcome by performance level

Learning outcomes	N	Mn	SD	Percent of responses by performance level (%)			
				High (3)	Moderate (2)	Low (1)	No (0)	Not submitted
1	24	2.3	0.8	45.8	33.3	20.8	0.0	0.0
2	24	2.0	0.9	37.5	29.2	33.3	0.0	0.0
3	24	2.0	0.7	25.0	54.2	20.8	0.0	0.0
All	72	2.1	0.8	36.1	38.9	25.0	0.0	0.0

Note: N = number of scores submitted; Mn = average score (mean); SD = standard deviation of scores.

levels than in the past but were less successful at identifying and defining basic concepts in historical analysis compared to their performance on learning outcomes. The assessment report excerpted in Table 1 and Figure 4 shows that of the 30 students enrolled in HIS 1610, 79.1 percent and 79.2 percent performed at the high or moderate level for the first learning outcome (describe the behaviors, practices, institutions, and/or systems that define a society or social group) and third learning outcome (analyze social institutions and social interactions), respectively.[3] These results correspond to data collected across the general education category overall. However, only 66.7 percent of students performed at the same level on the second learning outcome (identify and define basic concepts in social analysis). To some degree, this reflected a flaw in the design of the assignment chosen for the purpose of assessment, which has since been corrected to ask students more explicitly to identify relevant historical thinking skills. However, the results also suggested that the instruction had not consistently and explicitly engaged with specific skills throughout the course. This required a pedagogical adjustment in the way that classroom activities were designed and class discussions

---

3. The moderate level here is the target for assessment of the General Education Program, as that level aligns most closely with learning outcomes. Rubrics, further information about assessment, and program-level reports can be found on the General Education website: https://wayne.edu/engaging-gened/instructors/assessment.

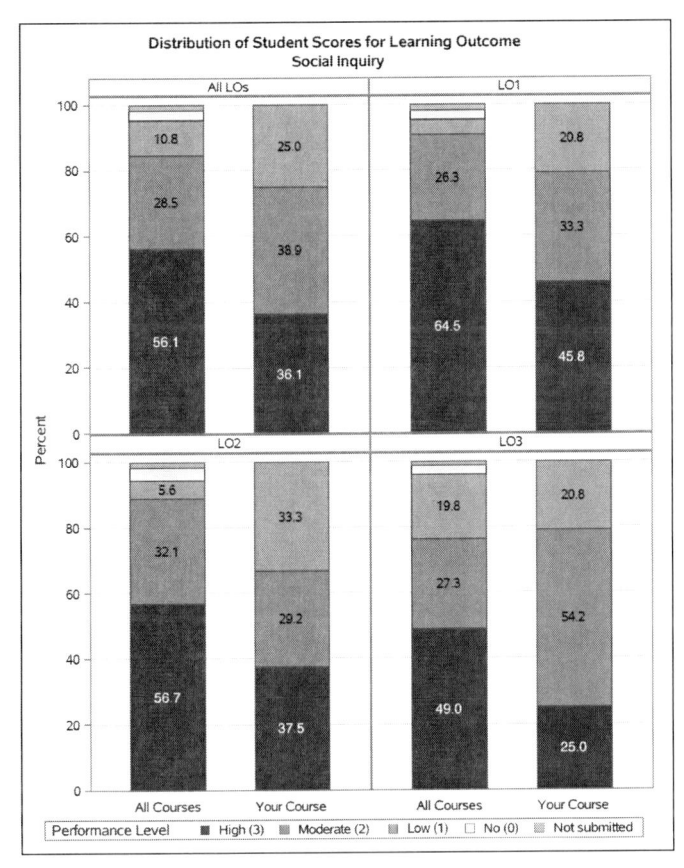

Figure 4. Comparison of learning outcomes by performance level.

organized.[4] Hart does not yet have a new assessment data point with which to weigh the relative effectiveness of this change, but she will continue to refine her approach in response to future data.

While the General Education Program assessment data presented here was not targeted at this particular project, and although its overall learning outcomes do not assess every goal

---

4. As part of the General Education Program Assessment Subcommittee, Hart produced an instructional video that walks through the process of reflecting on an assessment report using this example, available at https://wayne.edu/engaging-gened/instructors/usingassessmentreports. Videos demonstrating how to read assessment reports and full program-level reports can also be found on this site.

of this particular course, it points to the productive potential of more targeted assessment programs that specifically assess the effectiveness of these kinds of curricular changes to support student success, particularly when coupled with reflective teaching practice and learner-centered course design. It also highlights the possible uses of this form of curricular design and assessment to advance educational equity in both introductory general education courses and across the major.

CASE STUDY

TWO HALVES OF A WHOLE: REDESIGNING THE US HISTORY SURVEY FOR RELEVANCE, REFLECTION, AND ACCESS

Sandra Frink and Margaret Rung

ABSTRACT

At Roosevelt University, we focused our 2019 redesign of the two introductory US history courses (HIST 106: United States History to 1865; and HIST 107: United States History since 1865) by identifying ways to foster engagement and inclusion, stimulate intellectual curiosity, and eliminate barriers to success. We accomplished this by organizing our courses around themes, developing active learning in the classroom, and incorporating accessible learning strategies. Our efforts helped students build community in classes that welcome diverse perspectives and opinions without judgment and allowed for a deeper appreciation and understanding of the material. We will continue to assess our results, expanding our efforts to other courses in the discipline and to gateway courses across the university curriculum.

CHALLENGE

The mission, history, and current academic culture of our university inspired and informed our multiyear initiative to revise the history survey courses. Roosevelt University is a comprehensive, nonsectarian, urban university with a significant number of first-generation students. Founded in 1945 on the principles of inclusion and equity, Roosevelt's student body reflects the diverse working-class communities of Chicagoland.[1] We are currently

---

1. Roosevelt University's mission of social justice is rooted in its commitment to diversity, inclusion, and access, reinforced through education and progressive action on behalf of our students and the greater community, and dedicated to

designated a Hispanic-serving institution, with approximately 55 percent of our students identifying as nonwhite and 45 percent of undergraduates eligible for Pell Grants. The university has long welcomed nontraditional students, many of whom transfer from two- and four-year colleges, sometimes years after their initial matriculation. In 2017–18, 43 percent of new students in introductory history courses were classified as transfer students; many juggle outside responsibilities, such as jobs and family. In 2020, a merger between Roosevelt and Robert Morris University brought in more than 1,000 students who needed assistance navigating the institutional structure and culture of Roosevelt—just as we transitioned to remote learning due to the pandemic.[2] Finally, instructors at Roosevelt have become increasingly aware of and sensitive to the needs of neurodivergent students. A typical class at Roosevelt, in other words, includes students of differing ages, socioeconomic backgrounds, and life goals, as well as varied preparation, skill levels, and learning styles. Significantly, our student body's diversity and the university's identity as a social justice institution informed discussions about the history surveys under consideration during the Gateways to Completion (G2C) project.

This diversity enriches the classroom but also presents challenges to instructors. Over time, Roosevelt has developed a strong tradition of pedagogical reflection to enhance student success; even before the G2C project began, history faculty consulted with one another about classroom strategies. But because Roosevelt also places a high value on academic freedom and professorial autonomy, each survey tended to be treated as its own individual course rather than as part of a holistic introduction to the history program.

We also soon recognized that while we had addressed diversity in our classrooms by creating courses with inclusive *content*, we were less adept at addressing how our teaching methods achieved inclusivity. Assessments conducted using students' final exams revealed that overall student retention of content in the surveys was low. Comprehensive data on DFWI rates—the percentage of students

---

"shaping the world's next generation of socially conscious and ethical citizens and leaders." "Our Story," Roosevelt University, accessed May 15, 2024, https://www.roosevelt.edu/about/our-story.

2. Robert Morris University (RMU) was a private university in Chicago that offered associate's and bachelor's degrees. It merged into and became an experiential learning college within Roosevelt University in March 2020.

who receive a D or F grade, who withdraw from a course, or whose progress is recorded as incomplete—provided by our Office of Institutional Research for 2017–18 illustrated how these inconsistencies manifested across the surveys. History 106 (US History to 1865) and History 111 (World History to 1500) demonstrated lower DFWI rates than History 107 (US History since 1865), and significantly lower rates than History 112 (World History since 1500), at 5.6 percent, 5.4 percent, 8.3 percent, and 15.4 percent, respectively.[3] History 106 and History 111 also had higher numbers of first-year students, but lower percentages of these students received DFWIs than first-year students in History 107 and History 112.[4] In History 112, 27 percent of first-year students were unsuccessful in the course.[5] Comparatively speaking, the surveys had lower DFWIs than other gateway courses at Roosevelt or history survey courses at other institutions, but the uneven statistics challenged us to examine how we could provide a more consistent, enriching, and successful experience for our students across the surveys.

We began by having the two instructors most responsible for teaching the US history surveys meet to discuss course content and methodologies. First, we asked what we really want students to get out of the course before we asked what we need to do to get them there. If we were to see one of our students a few years after they took our US history survey course, we wondered, what would we want them to remember? Revolutionary War battles? Acronyms for the New Deal programs? We felt that history faculty too often present the US history survey as a compendium of facts delivered via lecture to students who must then recall them when prompted on exams. Students rightly deride the courses for

---

3. Roosevelt University's Office of Institutional Research provided only one year of DFWI data (2017–18). The inferences we can draw from one year of data are limited, nor were we able to compare data from pre- and post-G2C introductory history courses. Any such comparisons would have been difficult given the onset of the pandemic, which resulted in a shift to different modalities and introduced disruptions into students' lives. Further complicating comparisons was the integration of RMU into Roosevelt in March 2020.

4. Enrollment in these courses is average for introductory courses at Roosevelt; several reach the maximum for in-person classes of 40. Online courses are capped at 25.

5. History 112 always has a higher enrollment than the other survey courses because we offer more sections of it, including at least one online section. The higher number of sections also means that adjuncts more frequently teach the course than they do History 106, 107, or 111.

this very reason. The digestion of names and dates does little to stimulate their intellectual curiosity. Nor does it foster belonging or engagement, either with the material or with each other.

So we determined, first, to move away from the mastery of facts in favor of exploring broad, enduring themes and concepts that would allow us to grapple with both constancy and contingency. We chose themes that would resonate today, relate to Roosevelt University's social justice mission, and allow us to incorporate content in a more deliberate and reflective manner. In addition, we restructured our course to incorporate active learning and universal design principles with the goal of fostering intellectual empowerment through the development of key transferable skills.[6] These changes produced a student-centered classroom that promoted belonging and engagement by increasing student interactions with one another and granting them more power to direct discussions and activities.

Method

Explore Ideas and Themes: Our redesign started by identifying themes that resonated across time and offered multiple pathways and intersections for discussion and debate. For example, the theme Politics and Culture allows us to focus on policy but also—more broadly and theoretically—speaks to conceptions of power, identity, resistance, and reform. The Life and Labor theme highlights the worlds of ordinary people to consider how they precipitated change and how well-known historical events shaped their lives. Freedom and Unfreedom offers an intersectional analysis of the limits and possibilities of agency.

We vary the means by which we explore themes. In one course, each class session begins with a big open-ended question touching on one theme. "What did freedom mean to enslaved people?" animates our discussion of Reconstruction, while questions about how business owners and workers define freedom frames a conversation of the late Gilded Age. In another course, students

---

6. Faculty incorporated insights and assignments from the universal design for learning (UDL) framework, which strives to remove environmental barriers to learning and anticipate variability in students. By offering multiple means of engagement, representation, action, and expression, students become expert learners: motivated, resourceful, and goal-directed. CAST, the Center for Applied Special Technology, provides research and guidelines about UDL: https://www.cast.org/impact/universal-design-for-learning-udl.

take ownership of their learning by collectively defining the themes in different contexts, choosing the primary sources with which to explore each theme, collaborating with one another to make sense of the materials, and reflecting on how the process built confidence in their knowledge and abilities.[7] In both survey courses, we revisit each theme throughout the semester in our discussions of primary sources, analyze them in formative and summative assessments, and consider them in light of our own assumptions in reflection essays.

Engage in Active Learning to Develop Skills: In all sections, we replaced lectures with classroom activities to accomplish two related goals: increase student engagement, and strengthen their skills in critical analysis. The in-class activities allow students to learn from one another, strengthen their communication skills, and build community while simultaneously encouraging them to move beyond discussion to application. In US History to 1865, for example, students consider the ways we create historical narratives and shape collective memory by crafting proposals for public commemorations of important but divisive historical figures. These activities also engage them in source analysis, prompting them to compare what different sources reveal about the lived experience of historical events. Groups might analyze a slave narrative alongside a ship manifest from the Slave Voyages Database in one class, while comparing eyewitness accounts and newspaper articles about the Triangle Shirtwaist Factory fire in another.

Create an Accessible Environment: Our efforts to eliminate barriers to access and provide a more inclusive learning experience are ongoing. We use digitized primary sources and open-access materials such as *The American Yawp*, an open-source online textbook.[8] About half of the faculty are enrolled in a professional development course on equity in teaching, and they are

---

7. Examples of databases used in the course include: The Geography of Slavery, University of Virginia, http://www2.vcdh.virginia.edu/gos/index.html; Slave Voyages, Slave Voyages Consortium, https://www.slavevoyages.org/; and The Valley of the Shadow: Two Communities in the American Civil War, University of Virginia Library, https://valley.lib.virginia.edu/.

8. Joseph Locke and Ben Wright, eds., *The American Yawp*, 2 vols., updated for AY2022–23, accessed September 27, 2023, https://www.americanyawp.com. *The American Yawp* also comes in a print version, which currently costs $25 per volume: Locke and Wright, eds., *The American Yawp: A Massively Collaborative Open U.S. History Textbook*, 2 vols. (Stanford University Press, 2019).

now incorporating theories and practices such as universal design for learning (UDL) and transparent assignment design to reach all learners.[9] Our courses now promote engagement, comprehension, and expression by empowering students to elaborate on the meaning of themes, by incorporating diverse voices in our choice of sources, and by providing multiple pathways for demonstrating comprehension. This, too, is a work in progress. We regularly incorporate reflection, allowing students to consider, reevaluate, and express their ideas about the concepts we explore.

Outcomes

Our assessments reveal that we are achieving our goal of increasing transferable skills in synthesis, analysis, and reflection. Our revised approach cultivates student appreciation of diverse experiences and perspectives, historically and contemporaneously. Finally, these efforts have reignited our own engagement with the material and with one another, sparking dialogue and a shared course bank of pedagogical ideas and practices to apply in the classroom.

Qualitative Evidence: Qualitative evidence from the Learning Gains Surveys, which we began giving after implementing our initial changes, demonstrates that we have been successful in our efforts to provide an inclusive classroom conducive to learning.[10] The comments focus on three main outcomes:

1. Make Connections and Build Community: Our redesign began prior to the COVID-19 pandemic and continued through the semesters in which we moved to remote and online learning. Though challenging, our transfer of in-person active learning to online and remote spaces was instrumental in keeping

---

9. Transparent assignment design is an equitable teaching practice designed to build confidence, foster belonging, and develop skills. This assignment framework promotes an understanding of how we learn by explicitly laying out the purpose, task, and criteria for success. It is part of the Transparency in Learning and Teaching project (TILT Higher Ed), which also includes curricula frameworks, assessments, and strategic initiatives. See the Transparency in Learning and Teaching website at https://tilthighered.com/.

10. The Learning Gains Survey—developed by the Gardner Institute for the Gateways to Completion (G2C) project and administered to students enrolled in history survey courses midway through each semester—requested feedback about course activities and assignments, the pace of the course, the directions and support provided, and the student's comprehension and motivation to succeed.

students engaged. Prior to the pandemic, students noted the community-building results of in-class activities; during the semesters spent online, that community-building became a central feature of student reviews. References to active engagement recur in their comments, including the priority paid to helping students make connections with one another and providing ways for shy students to participate. One student noted, "This is my favorite class. She is my only teacher that really pushes interactions with my peers in class." Another noted that the activities made it "seem like we are in an in-person class."
2. Value of Different Voices: Students observed two ways that the expression of diverse voices enhanced their learning. First, they noted the value of learning from their peers. Working in groups allowed them to brainstorm, bounce ideas off each other, and learn from one another. Second, providing space for diverse voices ensured the expression of many different points of view. As one student reflected, "[I] liked hearing different opinions and ideas of my fellow classmates because we could have deep discussions . . . from different viewpoints." This approach fostered an environment in which students had "the opportunity to think freely without any judgment or negativity."
3. Comprehension and Deeper Understanding of the Material: The qualitative data suggests we are succeeding in providing opportunities for a deeper and more enriching engagement with the themes and ideas of the course. Students spoke of better understanding the material and gaining the confidence to express their interpretations and viewpoints. One student noted that the activities granted them the "space to talk about my thinking in small groups, where people can grow and build off each other's ideas." The result was a sense of ownership of the material: students felt comfortable exploring and debating ideas they found in assigned sources or issues beyond the classroom. Numerous students described continuing to research issues after the class ended, on their own time.

Quantitative Evidence: Quantitative data from the Learning Gains Survey, recorded every semester since spring 2019, confirm and elaborate on sentiments expressed in the qualitative data (Table 1). Results demonstrate that the US history survey course receives consistently strong scores overall, and especially in the categories of methodology, content, and comprehension. This likely reflects the fact that we began our revisions to the survey

Table 1. Average score/question for all sections of the US history survey, spring 2019 to spring 2022

	Semester/Year			
Questions	Sp19	F19–Sp20	F20–Sp21	F21–Sp22
The Class Overall				
How class topics, activities, and assignments fit together	4.4	4.15	4.2	4.15
Pace of class	4.1	3.8	4.1	4.1
Assignments, Graded Activities, and Tests				
Graded assignments (overall)	4.3	3.9	4.05	4.25
Number and spacing of tests	4.3	3.95	4.15	4.3
The way grading helped me understand what I need to work on	4.2	3.75	4	4.1
Feedback on tests and assignments	4.4	3.95	4.1	4.3
Information You Were Given				
Explanation of how class activities, reading, and assignments relate to each other	4.2	4.2	4	4.2
Explanation of instructor of how to learn and study	4.3	4.15	4.2	4.15
Explanation of why class focused on topics presented	4.1	4.05	4.15	4.2
Understanding of Class Content				
Main concepts	4.5	4.15	4.2	4.15
Relationship between concepts	4.3	4.1	4.2	4.25

Note: Response rates on the survey ranged from 50 to 95 percent of enrolled students. Enrollments in each section ranged from 27 to 41.

at the start of the G2C project. Scores remained at this high level through our period of remote learning during the pandemic (spring 2020 through spring 2021), indicating that students perceive the courses as cohesive, understand the connections between topics, and see the links between course objectives and assessments. All of this translates into comprehension and retention of the main concepts.

The Future

Our goals going forward are threefold: to further develop our course banks, to assess how these changes impact student performance and engagement in our upper-division courses, and to conduct dialogues about pedagogy with department colleagues and across the university.

We created our course banks to share learning objectives, assignments, rubrics, and sources with one another when we began these revisions. We are now coordinating workshops to discuss experiences using these resources and develop best practices that can be applied across sections and survey topics. Recently, we convened to discuss research on how we might refine our use of reflection assignments in the history survey and other courses. We are planning additional workshops that will focus on how we can further apply UDL and other accessible learning principles to our curriculum.

We also plan to develop assessments of our upper-division courses that will gauge learning transfer from the surveys to more focused courses. This will allow us to ascertain whether focusing on ideas and critical thinking skills rather than strictly on content prepares students for the rigors of upper-division analysis, and how to build upon these skills effectively.

Finally, we continue to take advantage of our colleagues' commitment to equitable teaching practices.[11] History faculty have taken an active role in shaping the conversation across the university in symposia, workshops, and lectures about ways to

---

11. The promotion of equitable teaching practices is part of the university's diversity, equity, and inclusion commitment, which also includes student engagement and support services, precollege access programs, and other initiatives designed to support the university's mission and the population it serves. "Diversity, Equity, and Inclusion: Resources," Roosevelt University, accessed May 15, 2024, https://www.roosevelt.edu/dei-resources.

ensure student success. We served on the committee that redesigned the general education and mission-related core as well as participating, more recently, in the university-wide Equity Teaching Academy. We wish to open future dialogues about the relevance of student learning outcomes in introductory-level courses to success in varied disciplines at the upper-division levels.

Lessons Learned

Our redesign allowed us to bring new life to the US history survey by incorporating enduring themes and redesigning student engagement with the material and with one another. When we began the G2C project, we did not anticipate the disruptions and challenges we would face due not only to the pandemic but also to the integration of another institution with Roosevelt, which occurred just as we shifted to remote learning. Neither of these developments halted our efforts, but they forced us to consider how to accomplish our goals online and remotely while assisting students who transitioned into Roosevelt without much notice. These disruptions emphasized the benefits of UDL, which suggested flexible ways to meet the varying needs of students. It also led to fruitful experimentation that we plan to continue. Even so, the movement between remote and in-person learning, along with the distinctive events of the last few years, made correlating our revisions to student performance impossible. Consequently, we are still gathering consistent data from each modality (online, remote, in-person) to determine what is working and what needs refinement. We encourage even the instructors who do not embrace a thematic approach or adopt all of our learning strategies to collaborate and reflect on their introductory courses, seeing each as a thread in a larger tapestry. While aspects of our experience or context may be unique, our approaches are transferable to other institutions. Even small modifications can make a profound difference in the experiences of students, contributing to their sense of community and their ability to achieve learning goals.

Themes and Variations

CASE STUDY

BUILDING STUDENT ENGAGEMENT IN HISTORY LABS

Elizabeth Hyde and Jonathan Mercantini

ABSTRACT

At Kean University, we have pioneered the incorporation of History Labs into the curriculum as both physical and metaphorical spaces in which students conduct historical research at William Livingston's 18th-century estate, Liberty Hall, and in Kean's Special Collections Research Library and Archives (SCRLA). Undergraduate scholars participate in large-scale collaborative research projects exemplified by our NEH-funded project, Make History@Kean: William Livingston's World. We sought to extend this model to History 1062: Worlds of History, a general education course required of all Kean students, by drawing on local archival manuscripts to teach global histories while encouraging student engagement and success.[1]

CHALLENGE

Worlds of History became required of all Kean students during a 2013 course redesign, which integrated more discussion and student projects into the classroom. But too much emphasis on content coverage—at the expense of skill building—made teaching the history of the world (from Plato to NATO) in a single semester nearly impossible. For Gateways to Completion (G2C), we took advantage of the design and creation of a new

---

1. The creation of HIST 1062 was a collaborative process including Sue Ellen Gronewold and C. Brid Nicholson. We thank the Kean instructors who have worked with us on the Gateways project, including Jamie Boszko, William Carr, Michael Carter, Camille Dantzler, Jessica DiFranco, Sean Dineen, Robert Hardmond, Thomas Henry, Matthew Iannucci, Christopher Irovando, Sue Kozel, Sean Nepveu, Stephen Price, Patricia Riak, Hector Santiago, Steven Shaffer, and Christiane Warren. The course is currently being revised under the leadership of department chair C. Brid Nicholson to align with new university curricular mandates.

building on campus for the Department of History that would also house Kean's SCRLA. By incorporating a classroom environment into the archives, we reimagined archival research as a History Lab.

At 14.7 percent, our 2017–19 DFWI rates in this course were lower than the national averages identified in Andrew K. Koch's "Many Thousands Failed" in 2017.[2] Still, based on that work and our understanding of the struggles students faced, we wanted to incorporate more and better active learning to increase student engagement in the course. In addition, we recognized the opportunity to combine concepts from our NEH-funded project, Make History@Kean, to better acquaint our students with world history ideas and how they connected to their own lives and campus. As a majority-minority and federally designated Hispanic-serving institution, we recognized the need to connect the study of world history to our students' lives and to the issues of social justice at the center of contemporary American culture.

Faced with the challenge of implementing best practices across 30 independent sections in the context of COVID-19, history department faculty created a standard course syllabus for all sections, the vast majority of which are taught by part-time instructors. While some instructors preferred having the freedom to create their own syllabi, standardization provided an opportunity to implement the History Lab concept using local history content to teach national and international events, along with other active learning assignments across every section.

Method

To achieve these goals, we introduced three primary source–based assignments rooted in local histories. First, a semester-long Migration Story assignment first introduced by Kean professor of history Sue Gronewold required students to explore the history of the world as the movement of peoples and write the migration story of themselves or someone close to them in the context of world history. Second, a unit on World War II was reorganized around a digitized set of 800 letters written by students and

---

2. Andrew K. Koch, "Many Thousands Failed: A Wakeup Call to History Educators," in this volume. DFWI rates refer to the percentage of students who received a D or F grade, withdrew from a course, or earned an incomplete.

alumni from Newark State Teachers' College (Kean's predecessor) who served in the war.[3]

Most importantly, we used local history sources to teach the Atlantic slave trade. Drawing on documents in the SCRLA and on the expertise of head archivist Erin Alghandoor, as well as digitized sources in other repositories, we built the still-evolving site William Livingston's World to share primary sources related to persons enslaved by the Livingston and Kean families, on whose estate our campus is built.[4] Guiding students through these documents while creating space for them to reach their own conclusions about slavery and the slave trade allowed them to better understand the history of the slave trade as well as the specific lives and labor of enslaved people on what is now their university campus. Documents were further supplemented by Kean professor of history C. Brid Nicholson discussing her research on enslaved men and women in the Livingston and Kean households.[5]

OUTCOMES

Our unit on the Atlantic slave trade—using primary source documents from our archives, filled with names our students recognize—made this history more accessible. As one instructor wrote, "This is a very effective and very relatable way of teaching slavery." The digitized documents, supplemented by methodological introductions to aid students in their analysis, ranged from lists of names of the enslaved scribbled on a lumber receipt to manumission agreements by which an enslaved husband and wife signed with an "X" in agreeing to salaried labor for the remainder of their lives. Eighty-six percent of students indicated that they liked working with scans of original manuscripts, and as shown in Figure 1, 88 percent of instructors responded positively when asked whether "teaching the history of slavery using these documents expanded student understanding." Figure 2

---

3. See the Nancy Thompson World War II Scrapbook Project, accessed September 25, 2023, https://www.kean.edu/history/make-history-kean/nancy-thompson-world-war-ii-scrapbook-project.

4. William Livingston's World, accessed September 25, 2023, https://sites.google.com/kean.edu/williamlivingstonsworld/history-lab-teaching-with-livingston/teaching-the-history-of-slavery-and-enslaved-persons.

5. See "HistoryTalks@Kean Community Forum," March 31, 2021, https://www.youtube.com/watch?v=gLpQL1TtSBE.

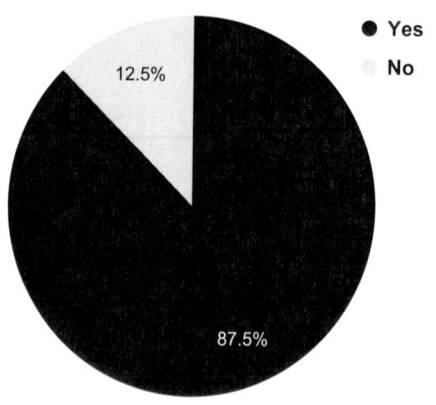

Figure 1. Does teaching the history of slavery using these documents expand student understanding of the history of slavery?

reveals that prior to completing this unit, more than half of Kean students—who are overwhelmingly from New Jersey—did not know that the institution of slavery existed in New Jersey.

One instructor felt these documents enabled students to "more fully empathize with people that had to endure" enslavement, while another noted that this assignment allowed students "to see that slavery existed in the North." Several students expressed sentiments similar to the student who said, "It [reading primary documents] made it feel more real." Another added, "I felt like it brought me closer to their experience and the evil that they had

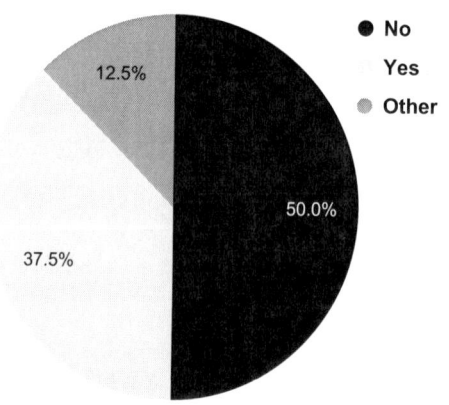

Figure 2. Did students generally know that the institution of slavery existed in New Jersey prior to working with these documents?

Spring 2022 through Spring 2023

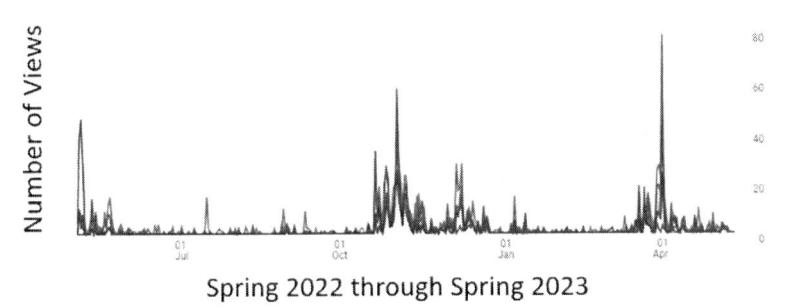

Figure 3. Number of views, March 2021 to May 2022.

to endure." Chosen carefully, even documents written by slaveholders can help convey the life experiences of enslaved men and women.

Through this deeper examination into the place of slavery in the Kean and Livingston families, students were able to better understand the history of slavery in the Americas. Students surveyed demonstrated a preference for reading primary over secondary sources and were most engaged by documents related to enslaved peoples. Importantly, the documents led them to conclude that, contrary to their preconceptions, the institution was not confined to the South and the Confederacy but had roots in the soil on which they now studied. At the same time, this curriculum underscored how US history in its entirety cannot be understood without the history and legacies of slavery. One instructor concluded, "This is such a powerful way of teaching slavery. Student engagement is high with this lesson."

Usage metrics for William Livingston's World (Fig. 3 and Table 1) demonstrate students engaged with seven primary sources each, averaging over five minutes per document.[6]

Through this unit, every Kean student (7,500 students to date) is introduced to the history of enslaved persons through the names and lives of those enslaved by the Kean and Livingston families. It is our hope that as we collectively acknowledge and confront this history, we can achieve a more inclusive and just future.

---

6. William Livingston's World, accessed September 25, 2023, https://sites.google.com/kean.edu/williamlivingstonsworld/history-lab-teaching-with-livingston/teaching-the-history-of-slavery-and-enslaved-persons.

Table 1. Website usage metrics

Metrics	Count
Views	6,087
Users	773
Views per user	7.87
Average engagement time (min:sec)	5:22
Event count	18,550

Impact

By allowing students to "do history" in the History Lab, our course redesign increased student engagement with challenging material. While some documents in the History Lab are transcribed, many are scans of original manuscripts, a feature preferred over transcriptions by instructors (87.5 percent to 12.5 percent) and a sentiment shared by 75 percent of students, who found the documents interesting (if challenging). A majority of students were more interested in or excited about these documents (62 percent) than the textbook (37 percent).

Building on this successful course redesign, we have incorporated History Lab into a number of other courses. Students in the History Honors Program and many of those taking the History Senior Seminar capstone course have developed and contributed their own findings—based on local primary sources—through essays, K–12 learning units, podcasts, and digitizing data. These have been shared as posters and oral presentations at Kean's annual Research Days as well as at regional and national conferences, including the 2020 American Historical Association annual meeting. These collaborative original research projects provide excellent preparation for students applying to and then succeeding in graduate school.

We also demonstrated History Lab to a group of K–12 teachers at our first Liberty in the American Revolution teachers' symposium, held at Kean in May 2022. Teachers had the opportunity to work with original sources connected to state standards, learn best and high-impact practices for using primary sources in the classroom, and devise their own lessons—all activities aimed at creating more just and inclusive classroom content and learning outcomes.

Lessons Learned

Kean is uniquely situated: with a physical history "lab" in the archives, and a campus built on an estate whose owners acquired wealth through the institution of slavery. Still, the underlying concept can be applied to other institutions: using primary source documents that speak to the local, the land, or the region students know (or think they know!). Place-based education is a demonstrated high-impact practice that improves student connections to the community and their commitment to good citizenship. And by creating an archive, be it physical or virtual, the lab work of historical thinking and primary source analysis can be infused into any course and curriculum. One Kean History 1062 instructor put it succinctly with regard to teaching the history of slavery through local sources: "the primary source material brought the situation to life." History Lab, another noted, "is very effective because of the personal connection that one gets with other people through primary documents."

The collaborative History Lab model resulted in a curriculum that builds both historical thinking and analytical skills while speaking to individual student interests, social justice demands, and the urgency of our moment. Funded by a grant from NEH Humanities Initiatives at Hispanic-Serving Institutions, we have shared these materials widely. By keeping the user interface simple and using readily available software such as Google Sites, we—and more importantly, our students—built a resource that will continue to expand as more content is created and additional source materials come to light.

CASE STUDY

BRINGING GROUP RESEARCH TO THE LARGE LECTURE HALL

Kelly Hopkins

ABSTRACT

The University of Houston (UH) is recognized as a leading research institution (R1) by the Carnegie Foundation. It is also designated as a Hispanic-serving institution (HSI) and an Asian American and Native American Pacific Islander–serving institution (AANAPISI). The university ranks second in the nation for diversity at a research institution and serves a minority-majority student population. Out of approximately 38,000 undergraduates, nearly half are classified as first time in college (FTIC) students. The state of Texas requires all students to pass two survey courses in American history to fulfill the requirements of a bachelor's degree. Most UH students complete this requirement with HIST 1301 (History of the United States to 1877) and HIST 1302 (History of the United States after 1877). These courses are taught in a variety of formats, including three hours of lecture in a large auditorium; a combination of two hours in a large lecture and one hour in smaller discussion classes (led by graduate student teaching assistants); and online synchronous or asynchronous delivery. This case study documents the development and implementation of a group research project to improve student success in sections with a large lecture component.

CHALLENGE

Enrollment caps in most introductory history courses at UH range from 270 to 360 students, with approximately 75 percent of the students in their first year (50 percent) or second year (25 percent) of college. These students are still learning the study strategies and time-management skills essential for classroom and college success. End-of-semester course evaluations reveal that more than

70 percent of enrolled students are pursuing a major outside of the College of Liberal Arts and Social Sciences. Most importantly, fewer than 1 percent of students are history majors, and 90 percent confess to enrolling in the course only because Texas requires it. Internal department data from the early 2010s reveal a clear correlation between courses with higher enrollments and rates of D, F, W, and I grades: a lack of interest in lectures, readings geared toward exams, and the sense of anonymity conjured by large auditoriums left students uninspired and disengaged from the course content and materials. The environment contributed to higher absentee rates, more missed assignments, and lower grade performance. Student struggles in gateway courses have a ripple effect on student retention rates, adding time to degree completion.

Knowing the impact that low student engagement has on classroom and degree-plan success, I targeted my course redesign at students on the lower end of the performance scale in HIST 1301 (History of the United States to 1877), a course taught face-to-face through lecture and discussion sections. I focused on increasing student engagement with course material and assignments, increasing student attendance, building skills that can be applied beyond the history classroom, and reducing the number of DFWI grades. I made changes to course pedagogy, structure, and curriculum while adopting high-impact teaching practices to create a more inclusive, equitable, and supportive classroom experience in which students could build a collaborative learning environment, practice the work of historians, and see themselves in a historical narrative.

When students returned to campus in fall 2021 following a full year of COVID-induced online instruction from fall 2020 to spring 2021, the need to build student support networks into the course structure only increased in urgency: these networks can help students navigate the rigorous demands of university expectations, contribute to positive mental health outcomes, create a sense of belonging in the university environment, and strengthen engagement with course materials throughout the semester. The pedagogical redesign emphasized active and experiential learning through a group research project that engaged students directly with historical events and evidence. Changes to the course structure provided flexibility and student choice in completing a major course requirement, as well as scaffolding skill development of key learning outcomes.

Method

The HIST 1301 course redesign adopted a group research project with five students collaborating on a historical topic or problem of their choice. Students worked independently and with their groupmates on scaffolded assignments to develop the larger project. Early in the semester, students narrowed down broad and wide-ranging topics into specific themes or events and divided into research groups. Research topics included: the ways different Indigenous nations responded to settler colonization, freedom seekers in Texas, the impact of technological advancements on westward expansion, immigrant experiences in different regions, and social, political, and resistance movements. To help students distill large ideas into manageable topics, they read two chapters from *The Craft of Research*, viewed research lesson videos, and completed information literacy lessons through the university library's website.[1] After students narrowed their topics, university research librarians visited the lecture hall to demonstrate navigating the library's catalog and searching for primary and secondary sources through popular databases like Academic Search Complete, JSTOR, newspapers, and Google Scholar. They also offered cautionary tales about the use of artificial intelligence (AI) tools such as ChatGPT. Students completed worksheets during the preliminary stages of research that guided their subsequent efforts to find relevant academic sources and brainstorm with group members on the focus and trajectory of their larger project as well as its historical significance.

Students employed search guidelines and tips from the librarians to locate at least four primary sources and two secondary sources relevant to developing their research projects during two separate weeks around the middle third of the semester. They submitted written reports reflecting on how they found a particular source and why they chose it, providing critical analysis of their sources and evidence, evaluating the reliability of their sources, and detailing how their sources would contribute to

---

1. Wayne C. Booth, Gregory G. Colomb, Joseph M. Williams, Joseph Bizup, and William T. Fitzgerald, *The Craft of Research* (University of Chicago Press, 2016), chaps. 3 4.

their portion of the group research project presentation. When written submissions revealed common struggles, we turned those roadblocks into learning opportunities in lecture. Students unable to locate the right primary sources on their own could revisit academic search engines as a group, look for appropriate sources, and share (via Mentimeter polling) online databases they found useful in their research. Online polling also provided a platform for students to anonymously share concerns or struggles that could then be addressed in class. Students developed the analytical skills to evaluate the reliability of sources through scaffolded think-pair-share exercises following individual work in lecture. During class time, students shared their sources and evidence with groupmates as their larger projects began to take shape. The collaborative assignment culminated in a 15-minute formal presentation delivered by each group during the last third of the semester. Students have flexibility in the format of their presentation, but all groups have used a traditional PowerPoint slide deck and oral presentation.

Although the project was a collaborative effort, students were graded individually at every stage of the process, beginning with three submitted worksheets; two research reports in the middle stages; two self- and peer evaluations of contributions to class meetings and research in the middle and final stages; and, lastly, their final presentation. Students received specific rubrics for each aspect of the project outlining the criteria for grades of Proficient, Competent, Novice, Standard Not Met, and No Submission. All assignments and rubrics were discussed in advance of due dates to ensure students understood my expectations and their responsibilities.

The numerous graded individual assignments and peer evaluations underscored the individual grade for the project rather than the group's collaboration. Nonetheless, student comments in their self-evaluations and peer evaluations highlighted an increased sense of accountability to their research partners because the team depended on them to fulfill their responsibilities to the final project.

Outcomes

The adoption of a collaborative group research project effectively engaged students with historical thinking, developed their ability to evaluate primary sources and historical evidence through scaffolded assignments, taught them to support historical arguments with the most relevant evidence, and employed metacognitive activities that required them to reflect on their own preparation, contribution, and study strategies. The variety of subject areas increased the diversity and inclusivity of course content—as students investigated historical topics of personal and even familial interest—while increasing empathy and an awareness of the perspective of others. Additionally, the group research project developed the essential soft skills that will contribute to student success across the university and in future careers. In working with new classmates on a collaborative project, students noted their improved communication and time-management skills as well as their dedication to a common goal as they worked together as a team. Students also valued the experience of creating and delivering a formal presentation as a critical component of future courses and careers. Most importantly, by creating a mini-learning community within the classroom, the group project provided an essential support system for first-generation students emerging from two years of mixed-learning pandemic-era platforms. Students engaged both with the historical material and with their classmates throughout the semester, felt an obligation to complete assignments because the group depended on their contribution, and learned from one another how to navigate the expectations of a university curriculum.

The group research project replaced a four-to-six-page paper as a course requirement. Data from fall 2018 and fall 2019 were used for evaluating the outcome of the course redesign (fall 2020 was not included because of alternate instruction modes during the pandemic). The group research project included several weeks of independent student research and writing, working with groupmates during class time, the formal presentation, and self-evaluations and peer evaluations reflecting on their weekly contributions to the total project; grades for the group project were based on these steps. Consequently, the course revision included multiple assessments rather than a single paper submission. This strategy ensured students could readily rebound after a bad week or one low grade.

When compared with the formal paper submissions, the data highlights both a significant improvement in the number of students earning A range grades (over 40 percent of students) and a

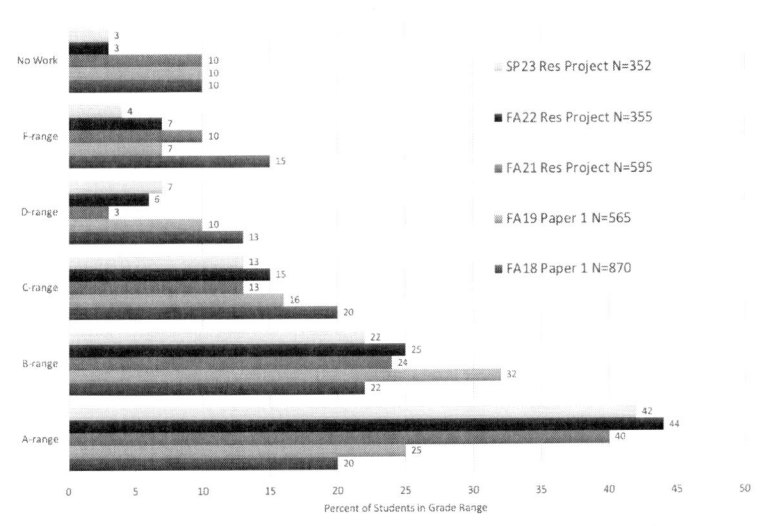

Figure 1. G2C course redesign for fall 2021, fall 2022, and spring 2023, with a group research project replacing the paper assignment used in fall 2018 and spring 2019. (The fall 2020 and fall 2021 semesters were not included due to COVID-19 instructional changes.)

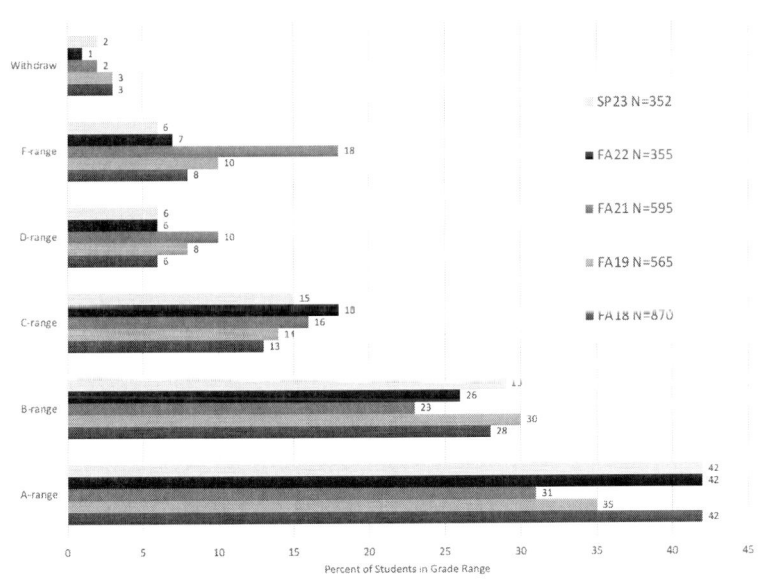

Figure 2. Course letter grades in fall 2018 and 2019 with a paper assignment, and fall 2021, fall 2022, and spring 2023 with a group research project.

reduction in the number of students falling into the D, F, and No Work submitted grade ranges (hovering around 5 percent over the last two semesters). In addition, 64 percent of students earned a grade of B– or higher, reflecting student comprehension of key course learning outcomes and skills. The data for course letter grades also show fewer students falling into the DFWI grade ranges, a primary goal of the course redesign. When the group research project was first implemented in fall 2021, students were faced with challenges from the ongoing pandemic and fluctuating delivery modes of course instruction. These realities complicated the full return to in-person instruction, impacted the level of student engagement with course materials and attendance, and resulted in high D and F rates. Course grades for fall 2022 and spring 2023 reflect both a reduction and a stabilization in the low-end grade ranges.

THE FUTURE

The group research project accomplished multiple course redesign objectives: it reduced the rates of D, F, and No Work Submitted grades; it engaged students with the work of historians; it made the course more inclusive to student interests; and it created a sense of community capable of providing a foundation for student well-being and success in university. Although they expressed anxiety about delivering formal presentations, the students practiced valuable skills—communication, initiative, time management, and teamwork—that will transfer well beyond the history classroom.

This redesign targeted small discussion sections capped at 30 students and can be incorporated seamlessly into upper-division and smaller-enrollment classes. The project will now be applied to a large lecture hall, with more than 300 students and without the small discussion sections. During the first weeks of the semester, students will choose their research topic from a set of 10 to 15 options. The logistical challenges of the formal presentations will be handled by assigning groups to record their presentations on Microsoft Teams or the learning management system; students will then provide formal feedback to at least five other presentations. Lecture days will still be used to introduce students to primary and secondary sources, build the skills necessary to evaluate different forms of historical evidence, and allow research librarians to show students how to navigate the library's website, research tools, and helpful scholarly databases. In addition, lecture days dedicated to the group research projects will give students space to discuss their sources and develop projects with their partners. Finally, students will have quick access to instructors to ask any questions, seek guidance on relevant sources, and ensure that their project has a research rather than a narrative focus. When fall 2021 began, the teaching assistants and I had no idea if the research project would be a hit or a terrible miss. We have been very happy with the level of student engagement, the range of interesting sources they located, and the supportive classroom they created together.

Lessons Learned

With three semesters of successful student research presentations now complete, future classes can be geared toward challenges navigating the library website, conducting preliminary research more efficiently, and identifying helpful internet databases on popular research subjects and potential primary sources. Previous student presentations can provide models for the planning, organization, and final delivery of the group research project. A primary goal moving forward is to identify students who are inconsistent in their preparation, contribution, and engagement with the assignment and try to help them complete the course successfully.

TEACHING REFLECTION

TAKING A THEMATIC APPROACH WITH THE HISTORY OF FUN

Sara Rzeszutek

On June 18, 1894, the *Salt Lake Herald* included a two-paragraph article consisting chiefly of a quote from the cycling magazine the *Wheel* about what women wear when they ride bicycles. "The Girl Cyclist in Bloomers" lays bare the gender anxieties of the 1890s. Cycling bloomers, or any new style of pant designed to improve women's comfort and mobility, "so much obscures the sex division that the urchin is compelled to assert that 'them's women!'" The author offers an alternative, more appropriate fashion choice. A bloomer that was "gracefully full and womanly wide," with only "a chic suggestion of trouser," would help women riders to be "pretty and apparently clever."[1] For a trained historian, a short article like this not only opens the door to further inquiry on gender anxieties, changing fashions, or the comparative popularity of cycling. It also provides a window onto shifting politics and economies, industrialization, and the broader cultural transformation underway as the 20th century approached.

In my gateway course History of the United States since 1896, I always open with this article. Students tend to focus initially on the two surface issues: women on bikes, and women's attire. But as I push them to dig deeper, and as I demonstrate how a historian might ask questions about the piece, we end up discussing a range of interconnected issues, such as how industrialization fueled the growth of a new middle class whose members led a more sedentary work life and took up health-related hobbies like cycling as a result, thereby transforming leisure industries and

---

1. "The Girl Cyclist in Bloomers," *Salt Lake Herald* (Utah), June 18, 1894, accessed September 13, 2022, Chronicling America: Historic American Newspapers, Library of Congress, https://chroniclingamerica.loc.gov/lccn/sn85058130/1894-06-18/ed-1/seq-3/.

related commerce. We also consider how economic and workplace changes fueled activism for women's rights, temperance, and other concerns of the early Progressive Era. Something as simple as the concern over women's attire and hobbies offers students a new way to understand the deeply interconnected facets of American life.

When I began considering ways to revise my course as part of our institution's participation in the History Gateways project, I wanted to build around the most successful modules in my class. Our introductory session on "The Girl Cyclist in Bloomers" was the first that came to mind. I considered what worked about it and why. Did it teach students historical thinking skills and critical analysis? How did it differentiate college-level history from their high school experiences? When students left the first session, were they more curious about what a history class could offer? Because the use of small-scale issues and events to explain larger trends seemed key, I decided to reorganize my course around a single theme and examine multiple periods through that lens.

The history of fun offered an ideal thematic framework for my course redesign. Researching for this revision revealed that "fun" was never simply a diversion. Instead, as the historian Carroll Pursell writes, "the democratisation of society created a mass market for the kind of amusements that could provide relief and distraction from the consumers everyday lives, played out in factories, shops, and tenements."[2] In other words, leisure in the United States was intimately tied to social, political, economic, and industrial change. I reviewed my existing syllabus and rebuilt it using readings, podcasts, and assignments focused on fun and leisure as entry points for exploring the chronology of events in a standard US history survey. I focused on works that would be accessible to students who had no experience engaging with academic work and found a wide assortment of primary and secondary sources in multiple formats around which to design my course. The redesigned syllabus now explores major developments in modern US history by asking how people from a range of backgrounds had fun.[3]

---

2. Carroll Pursell, "Fun Factories: Inventing American Amusement Parks," in "Playing with Technology: Sports and Leisure," special issue, *Icon* 19 (2013): 75–99.
3. Samples of academic articles used in my class with corresponding JSTOR Daily pieces: Judy Kutulas, "'That's the Way I've Always Heard It Should Be':

Entertainment and leisure trends frequently reflect how regional, national, and international events influenced the everyday lives of ordinary Americans. Those same trends shed light on who embraced fun in what ways—and who was excluded or lacked access to that fun—which allows us to explore changing experiences of race, gender, class, region, and religion. This approach draws students into the material in a different way than the more traditional survey course that I've taught for many years. It opens the door to thinking directly about how historians form questions and interpret sources, because the thematic focus demands complex thinking about history both as a practice and as a factor in our present lives. Its inherent interest to students hones their curiosity and engagement—even among students who have long dreaded taking a required history course. My course redesign inspired transformations in my pedagogical approach and also later informed part of our institution's revision of its general education program.

COURSE STRUCTURE AND PEDAGOGY

Reorganizing a gateway-level course around a theme like fun requires rebuilding a standard course from the ground up. The process itself was fun! But I wanted to ensure that my pedagogical changes were also driven by data, research into student learning and history instruction, and my own experiences and observations. I was confident that my course was engaging and that students were learning, but I also sought to foster equity, inclusion, and feeling connected to the past. I also wanted to break out of the traditional textbook-oriented narrative, which students routinely perceive as "boring." Providing a range of students—from those who were underprepared in university history courses to those with a strong foundational knowledge—with an interesting and outside-the-box approach to how historians work involved rethinking reading lists, written assignments, and my overall class structure.

Baby Boomers, 1970s Singer-Songwriters, and Romantic Relationships," *Journal of American History* 97, no. 3 (2010): 682–702; Mischa Honeck, "The Power of Innocence: Anglo-American Scouting and the Boyification of Empire," *Geschichte und Gesellschaft* 42, no. 3 (2016): 441–66; Mary Murphy, "Bootlegging Mothers and Drinking Daughters: Gender and Prohibition in Butte, Montana," *American Quarterly* 46, no. 2 (1994): 174–94; Brian Ward, "Civil Rights and Rock and Roll: Revisiting the Nat King Cole Attack of 1956," *OAH Magazine of History* 24, no. 2 (2010): 21–24.

In building out my course, I focused on understanding the purpose and significance of the gateway-level history course. As Andrew Koch noted in "Many Thousands Failed" in 2017, gateway history courses have staggeringly high DFWI rates. Success or failure in gateway history courses correlates with college retention rates overall, and these rates also break down along racial lines, confirming that introductory-level college courses play an important role in shaping long-term institutional demographics. Such courses can either perpetuate or mitigate the effects of racial inequality in higher education and beyond. Inclusive pedagogical practices, material that reflects the student body, and active learning can help change this dynamic.[4]

Aspects of traditional history instruction are undeniably important; still, as instructors we often have only one opportunity in a student's entire college career to help them see how methods of historical inquiry can be valuable and relevant. If students have felt alienated or intimidated by a barrage of facts, dates, names, and places—or excluded and unrepresented by the dominant narrative in their previous history instruction—then we do them a disservice by delivering a course experience that is simply a more challenging version of what they've already done. When students tune out of a course that seems irrelevant to them, they grow increasingly at risk of total disengagement or failure. Breaking away from the traditional course model helps address these concerns and set up students for success.

My redesigned course on the history of fun does not focus on the standard sequence of major topics. I don't worry, for instance, if there's no time to explain every detail of US involvement in World War I. This choice draws on Lendol Calder's work on "uncoverage," which reframes a survey course as an opportunity for students to learn about the past through active learning, rather than by having history "covered" by lectures.[5] While some scholars and educators express concern that moving away from a coverage-oriented approach hinders a student's ability to know the whole past, there is scant conclusive evidence that

---

4. See Andrew K. Koch, "Many Thousands Failed: A Wakeup Call to History Educators," in this volume.

5. Lendol Calder, "Uncoverage: Toward a Signature Pedagogy for the History Survey," accessed September 25, 2022, http://archive.oah.org/textbooks/2006/calder/index-2.html.

courses organized around a lecture and textbook-style narrative result in quality learning.[6] As Calder notes, content coverage limits an instructor's ability to guide students through the most exciting and important aspects of historical work, including the excitement of discovery, the development of interpretative and argumentative skills, and the necessary and relevant meaning that the past holds for students. Instead, he writes:

> When history is presented in this way, as a mass of facts to be absorbed by sponge-like minds, who can wonder at reports that the survey leaves most students feeling confused and unable to reconstruct what they have just studied. For the best students, taking the survey is like trying to get a drink from a fire hydrant. For most, it leaves entirely the wrong idea about what history really is.[7]

Teaching students to connect with the past through a thematic lens helps pique their curiosity and interest. Students curious enough to pursue a question are primed to understand historical methodology and develop the skills to find and interpret contextual information about the past. They may not leave the course ready to offer a complete and chronological narrative of US history, but they will know how to ask good questions and scrutinize the information they find when seeking answers. With a world of information readily available on the phones in their pockets, the tools of historical inquiry may hold more value than a series of facts, the retention of which will dissipate with time. After all, most students will take only one history course, but the skills they acquire will serve them over the course of their entire academic careers.

A thematic focus teaches students to zero in on a moment and build a larger conversation around it—situating the moment in context using historical inquiry and research methods. This approach equips them to become good historical thinkers and apply those skills in other courses. I have seen evidence that this approach is successful. Two years after taking my newly redesigned course, one student applied his knowledge to a religious

---

6. Lendol Calder, "The Best Result," accessed September 25, 2022, http://archive.oah.org/textbooks/2006/calder/pr_best.html.

7. Lendol Calder, "A Worse Result," accessed September 25, 2022, http://archive.oah.org/textbooks/2006/calder/pr_worse.html.

studies course. Commenting on a text about the history of musical worship within Judaism, the student wrote: "You can learn so much about the history of literally anything by focusing on a specific aspect of it. For example, Dr. Rzeszutek's class talked about American history through the lens of the entertainment industry and much of the history of the country could be extrapolated from the pieces we worked on in that class. Similarly, here worshippers learned about Judaism simply through music. I think that's a wonderful thing."[8] This student was able to apply historical inquiry to another discipline with nuance and expansive thinking. And despite the effects of the COVID-19 pandemic, grades across the board in my remodeled course have been noticeably higher. There were fewer incomplete assignments, and students produced stronger work that showed more engagement with and excitement about the material.

The history of fun required that I move away from a textbook and opened the door to a wide range of niche readings, podcasts, and documentaries capable of offering students the connections I hoped to help them make. Many of the new readings came from *JSTOR Daily*. As I've discussed in a previous essay, *JSTOR Daily* articles are short, academically driven readings that focus on the most interesting parts of scholarly articles.[9] Pieces like "Boy Scouts and the Phenomenon of Boyification," "How Prohibition Encouraged Women to Drink," "Why MLK Believed Jazz Was the Perfect Soundtrack for Civil Rights," and "Woodstock: Sex, Drugs, and Zoning" provide free links to the scholarly articles on which they are based, so that students can read further if so inclined.[10] In addition, the brevity of *JSTOR Daily* pieces allows me to choose an assortment of articles for each period, giving students wider

---

[8]. Jenny Labendz shared the student's comments with the author in a screenshot on February 9, 2022; they are used with the student's permission.

[9]. Sara Rzeszutek, "Teaching U.S. History with JSTOR Daily," *JSTOR Daily*, January 5, 2021, https://daily.jstor.org/teaching-u-s-history-with-jstor-daily/.

[10]. Matthew Willis, "Boy Scouts and the Phenomenon of Boyification, *JSTOR Daily*, August 9, 2019, https://daily.jstor.org/boy-scouts-and-the-phenomenon-of-boyification/; Erin Blakemore, "How Prohibition Encouraged Women to Drink," *JSTOR Daily*, February 16, 2018, https://daily.jstor.org/how-prohibition-made-womens-drinking-more-acceptable/; Ashawnta Jackson, "Why MLK Believed Jazz Was the Perfect Soundtrack for Civil Rights," *JSTOR Daily,* October 16, 2019, https://daily.jstor.org/why-mlk-believed-jazz-was-the-perfect-soundtrack-for-civil-rights/; Matthew Willis, "Woodstock: Sex, Drugs, and Zoning," *JSTOR Daily*, May 9, 2019, https://daily.jstor.org/woodstock-sex-drugs-and-zoning/.

exposure to leisure trends over time. And selecting a variety of articles rather than a textbook chapter makes space for more inclusive content, helping to ensure that the perspectives of people with diverse identities are represented in assigned materials and giving more students more opportunities to connect with the past. For gateway-level students, exposure to academic ideas on a range of topics in short pieces proved more valuable than expecting them to read, digest, and apply knowledge from much longer academic essays or textbook chapters.

In addition to rethinking my reading list, I also rethought other course assignments. Because some students learn more effectively through audio or visual formats, I added podcast episodes, videos, and images throughout the course. Podcasts are especially popular, allowing students to complete assignments while doing other things or providing a break to those suffering from screen fatigue. One podcast—99% Invisible's episode "The Infantorium"—blends medical records, early 20th-century culture, and entertainment history by exploring the developments in neonatal care within the context of amusement park sideshows.[11] The episode not only offers a unique insight into a moment; it also surprises students with little prior interest in history. For science-oriented students, the episode contextualizes work they do in labs and encourages them to think about the progress medicine has made over time. The episode also spends significant time focused on Coney Island, which is interesting for our many students who grew up in Brooklyn. Local stories can connect students to the history under their feet; my students were able to compare the fun they'd once had at Coney Island to the experiences of people a century before.

Primary sources are central to any history course, but I use them more often for in-class, active learning rather than assign them for homework: older language, even language used just a few decades ago, can be challenging for students. On our first full day of class session after the introductory session, we explore the transition from a Gilded Age mentality about wealth to the Progressive Era. The Bradley Martin Ball, a lavish affair held at New York City's Waldorf-Astoria hotel in the midst of the 1897 economic depression, offers a window onto this change. Students had

---

11. "The Infantorium," *99% Invisible*, podcast, ep. 381, December 3, 2019, https://99percentinvisible.org/episode/the-infantorium/.

already learned about patterns of "conspicuous consumption," an expanding wealth gap, and laissez-faire economic values; controversy surrounding the ball reflected a transformation in ideas about how the very rich spent their money. Students broke into groups to read four different *New York Times* articles about the affair. Two articles focus on positive aspects of the ball, including preparations for floral arrangements, seating, rehearsals for the quadrille dance, and arguments that the spending would have a positive economic impact. The other two address criticisms—including arguments that wasteful spending was tasteless and out of touch—and discuss threats of violence against the Martin family. Students presented their articles and the class examined what they reveal as a set of sources about changing notions of wealth and leisure at the turn of the century. This exercise opens the door for subsequent discussions about the nature of social justice reforms, social control efforts, and other Progressive Era transformations in American life.

Another primary source that addresses leisure and connects to the course's broader themes is Theodore Roosevelt's 1899 speech "The Strenuous Life," which celebrates hard work, virtue, and "victorious effort." If a person misuses time spent away from work and "treats this period of freedom from the need of actual labor as a period not of preparation, but of mere enjoyment, he shows that he is simply a cumberer of the earth's surface, and he surely unfits himself to hold his own with his fellows."[12] The speech encourages Americans to reject "ignoble ease." Endorsing the nation's imperial turn, Roosevelt connected changing ideas about the role of "fun" to the responsibility of bringing "civilization" to new US possessions. Patiently breaking down this speech in class encourages discussion of its broader context and gives students space to engage in historical inquiry about changing attitudes in American culture.

Reworking my syllabus forced me to think about what students should know, understand, and be able to do at the end of a gateway course, and I wanted to find ways to assess their mastery of the skills and concepts central to historical thinking. I began by reevaluating the formal papers that required students

---

12. Theodore Roosevelt, "The Strenuous Life," speech delivered in Chicago, April 10, 1899, accessed September 24, 2022, Voices of Democracy: The US Oratory Project, https://voicesofdemocracy.umd.edu/roosevelt-strenuous-life-1899-speech-text/.

to integrate primary and secondary sources. This was an area where they felt pressure and frequently turned their focus to aspects of the assignment that lay outside of historical thinking; meanwhile, I struggled to separate my assessment of their history skills from the quality of their writing. For first-semester students with no foundational writing course under their belts and little experience with academic prose, measuring historical learning through such an assignment resulted in inequitable grading.

I have found that encouraging students to write first-person reflections about their thought process, the ideas that grabbed their attention, and why those things matter historically proves a better tool for seeing where learning is happening. Students tend to relax when they're allowed to be informal, which helps them stay open to the material itself and even to become better writers. Not only does a less formal process help students to find their own voice; it also reduces academic dishonesty by eliminating the anxieties around sounding a certain way on the page, a pressure that weighs on many students. The advent of AI technologies and ChatGPT offers further motivation for instructors seeking to revamp assignments and find ways for students to cultivate an authentic voice.

Offering multimodal assessment tools can help ensure that measurements focus on students' grasp of history methods and ideas, and not on other criteria. In one larger assignment, scaffolded over the course of the semester, students interview an older relative or community member about their memories of growing up and what they did for fun. The students are given oral history instruction and guidance on finding secondary sources to broaden their understanding of the period. They produce a podcast, digital exhibit, or other creative project based on that interview. They also write a short first-person reflection on the process. In podcasts, students connect with their interviewee in ways they may not have expected and begin to see that historical thinking has relevance beyond the classroom. Many of the creative projects draw on students' existing talents. One student produced a board game that transported players through his grandfather's urban upbringing. These types of assignments allow students to tap into their strengths as they showcase their historical thinking—to communicate their knowledge through podcasting, presentations, creative work, digital media, and papers—while giving me the chance to see their curiosity and understanding expressed through their own unique lens.

IMPLICATIONS FOR GENERAL EDUCATION

Shortly after launching my course redesign, I took on the role of faculty director of general education and was tasked with introducing changes to our existing general education program based on data-informed shortcomings and qualitative research into the success of our program. My course redesign experience through History Gateways and my background in the American Historical Association's Tuning the History Discipline project shaped my approach to revising the university's general education program.[13] These processes intertwined, highlighting how to reconceptualize my gateway course in the context of general education and use that thinking to inform the program's overall structure.

Our general education program includes a First Year College along with categories of learning called Bodies of Knowledge. In the revision, I proposed a reduction in course load to improve first-year completion rates and the addition of a learning-community component to help students develop applied learning skills. As of fall 2022, St. Francis College has launched learning communities linking Bodies of Knowledge courses to first-year courses in writing and public speaking across the first-year experience. My course is currently paired with a public-speaking course, which fits perfectly with assignments focused on oral history and podcasting, and I look forward to collaborating with another instructor to strengthen my course further.

Reworking my course was also relevant to revising the university's general education program because it required me to focus on how students understand the purpose and goals of each course component. This demand translates to general education as well. Qualitative data revealed that students (and some faculty) did not have a solid understanding of how the program worked or why certain requirements existed; in response, I rewrote the program descriptors to emphasize student-centered language. I removed heavily academic wording from the program and workshopped

---

13. "Tuning the History Discipline in the United States," American Historical Association, accessed October 3, 2022, https://www.historians.org/teaching-and-learning/tuning-the-history-discipline.

new descriptions with faculty across the college and with a student focus group. This process included a full revision of Bodies of Knowledge titles and learning outcomes. I also added a rationale that explained to students why each area of general education matters in their academic career and beyond. The fundamentals of the program remained largely the same, but our approach to communicating the structure and rationale to students shifted significantly. As I had with my own course, I took a step back from the program as it existed and thought about what kind of language would be most accessible to our students. Even if a course itself does not change, students will understand its purpose beyond simply checking a box on a list of requirements.

Revising general education helped me think about my own gateway course in a new context as well. As experts who have devoted our lives to an area of inquiry, it's normal to prize our discipline above all others and see our courses as essential to a student's education. But from the perspective of general education, each course or category serves an equally important purpose in developing thoughtful and broadly educated students. General education should benefit the student in their major field—whether that's nursing, philosophy, accounting, or history—while enabling them to build an expansive intellectual framework that fosters success in their careers and further education. Each gateway course should not only introduce the discipline-specific skills and knowledge necessary to advance in a major; these courses should also function as building blocks for applied learning, cross-disciplinary thinking, and whole-person education. In my History of Fun gateway course, I strive to give students—regardless of major or initial interest level—something relevant for their own path that they can take with them to other courses. Whether it's a new understanding for nursing students about how neonatal care developed in amusement parks, a fresh way for management students to look at the connection between industrialization and fashion, or simply a deeper curiosity among all my students about unexpected interconnections in the world around them, a general education gateway-level history course should be meaningful for every participant.

Redesigning my course around the history of fun rekindled my excitement for teaching. I go to class eager to share the period or topic under discussion and to help students use a narrow but stimulating lens to ask questions, building context and developing the skills essential to academic growth. The redesign stripped my gateway course of the monotony that had built up over the years and forced me to address the conflict I felt using a textbook, relying on lectures, and assigning formal essays. It also compelled me to understand why students took my class and shifted my focus to their broader academic needs as part of a general education program. It pushed me to be clear with students about why they're doing what they're doing and the expected outcomes—to revise the material, instructions, and explanations using student-centered language. I've become more experimental in the classroom and am confident that the history of fun is more equitable, inclusive, enlightening—and yes, *fun*—for all students.

Contributors

Julia Brookins is the senior program analyst, teaching and learning, at the American Historical Association, where she is part of the team that develops and implements initiatives to advance history in education and public life. She has a PhD in US history from the University of Chicago with a focus on immigration and citizenship in the Southwest.

Theresa Case earned her PhD at the University of Texas at Austin and has taught at the University of Houston–Downtown since 2002. Her publications include *The Great Southwest Railroad Strike and Free Labor* (Texas A&M Univ. Press, 2010) and "In the Trenches of World War I–Era Texas: Letters from Black Railroaders to the United States Railroad Administration" (*Southwestern Historical Quarterly*, 2021).

Celeste Chamberland is an associate professor of history and director of the history and international studies programs at Roosevelt University, where she teaches courses on world history, medical history, and race and gender in the Atlantic World. Her research interests include the history of surgical education and the history of addiction. Her publications include articles in *Social History of Medicine*, *History of Education Quarterly*, and *Sixteenth-Century Journal*.

Stephanie M. Foote is the vice president for teaching, learning, and evidence-based practices at the John N. Gardner Institute for Excellence in Undergraduate Education. Before joining the Gardner Institute, Stephanie was a professor of education, a faculty fellow for high-impact practices, and the founding director of the master of science in first-year studies at Kennesaw State University. Stephanie's research spans a variety of topics, including the role of first-year seminars and experiential pedagogy on student engagement, transfer students, self-authorship development, engagement in online environments, faculty development, metacognitive teaching and learning approaches, high-impact educational practices, and inclusive teaching.

Sandra Frink is an associate professor of history at Roosevelt University, where she serves as the chair of the humanities department and the director of the women's and gender studies program. She is a cultural and social historian whose recent research explores representations of gender and sexuality in popular culture during the 19th and early 20th centuries. She teaches a diverse range of courses on topics including the historical memory of the Civil War, gender and popular culture, creating community histories using oral history, and gender and race in the Atlantic World.

Jennifer Hart is a professor and department chair in history at Virginia Tech. She previously served as an associate professor of history and director of the general education program at Wayne State University. Hart is the North American president for the International Society for the Scholarship on Teaching and Learning in History and a senior scholar in the AAC&U's Office of Curricular and Pedagogical Innovation.

Kelly Hopkins is an assistant professor of early American history at the University of Houston. Her research interests include the fields of Native American, British, and French colonial American, environmental, and Atlantic World histories. She regularly teaches the American history survey to 1877, focusing on improving undergraduate education and student success.

Anne Hyde is David L. Boren Professor of History at the University of Oklahoma (OU) and editor of the *Western Historical Quarterly*. After earning a PhD in history at the University of California, Berkeley, she began teaching at Louisiana State University. She later joined the faculty at Colorado College, where she served for 22 years; there she directed the race and ethnic studies program, the Southwest studies program, and the Faculty Learning and Development Center. From 2011 to 2014, she served on the AHA Council as a member of the Teaching Division, and she is serving as vice president, Professional Division, in 2023–26. As faculty director of the AHA's Tuning project since 2012, she faced challenges of curricular reform and equitable teaching. At OU, she teaches the required introductory US survey in every format.

Contributors

Elizabeth Hyde is associate dean (acting) of the College of Liberal Arts and professor of history at Kean University. Her first book, *Cultivated Power: Flowers, Culture, and Politics in the Reign of Louis XIV*, explores the collection, cultivation, and political importance of flowers in early modern France. She is currently writing *Of Monarchical Climates and Republican Soil: Nature, Nation, and Botanical Diplomacy in the Franco-American Atlantic World*, an analysis of the North American mission of French botanist André Michaux. She held a Mellon Visiting Scholar Fellowship at the New York Botanical Garden, and her work has been recognized with funding from the NEH, American Philosophical Society, and NSF, as well as talks at the Metropolitan Museum of Art, Huntington Library, and American Philosophical Society. She is currently a senior fellow at Dumbarton Oaks and the editor of *Studies in the History of Gardens and Designed Landscapes*.

Michael Stelzer Jocks is an assistant teaching professor of history at Roosevelt University, where he teaches courses on world history, modern European history, sports history, and US history.

Andrew K. Koch is chief executive officer of the John N. Gardner Institute for Excellence in Undergraduate Education. A recipient of need-based aid while in school, Koch is a staunch advocate for and leader of efforts that increase student access to and completion of postsecondary education. He has worked in and with higher education institutions for over 30 years, including at the Gardner Institute since 2010. A historian by training, Koch began his career in education as a high school social studies teacher.

Jonathan Mercantini is acting associate provost for special projects and professor in Kean University's Department of History, where he has taught since 2007. He is a member of the New Jersey Historical Commission and a trustee of the New Jersey Council for the Humanities. His current research projects include Make History@ Kean: William Livingston's World, an exploration of the 18th-century Atlantic World funded by a Humanities Initiatives Grant from the National Endowment for the Humanities, and the Battles of Connecticut Farms and Springfield, funded by grants from the New Jersey Historical Commission and the National Park Service.

David Pace is a professor emeritus in the history department at Indiana University Bloomington. In addition to his work in

European history, he is the co-creator of the decoding the disciplines approach to increasing student learning and has published numerous works in the scholarship of teaching and learning, most recently *The Decoding the Disciplines Paradigm*. He was the 2004 recipient of the American Historical Association's Eugene Asher Distinguished Teaching Award and has been a fellow in the Carnegie Academy for the Scholarship of Teaching and Learning; he was also president of the International Society for the Scholarship of Teaching and Learning in History.

Kenneth Pomeranz is University Professor of History at the University of Chicago. His work mostly focuses on Chinese, comparative, and world history. He has written, edited, or coedited 11 books, including *The Great Divergence: China, Europe, and the Making of the Modern World Economy*, *The Making of a Hinterland: State, Society and Economy in Inland North China, 1853–1937*, and *The World that Trade Created* (with Steven Topik). He belongs to the American Academy of Arts and Sciences and the British Academy, was president of the American Historical Association in 2013, and has won the Dan David Prize and the Toynbee Prize for World History.

Sara Rzeszutek is professor of history and director of the Center for the Advancement of Faculty Excellence at St. Francis College. She previously served as the director of the honors and general education programs. Her scholarship focuses on the history of civil rights and Black radicalism, and she is the author of *James and Esther Cooper Jackson: Love and Courage in the Black Freedom Movement* (Univ. Press of Kentucky, 2015).

Margaret Rung is professor of history and director of the Center for New Deal Studies at Roosevelt University. Her scholarship and teaching explore 20th-century social and political history with an emphasis on the Great Depression and World War II.

Claire Vanderwood is a high school teacher based in Toronto, Canada. She earned a BA in history, with a focus on colonial North America, from George Washington University in 2021. From 2021–22, she was the program assistant, academic and professional affairs, at the American Historical Association.

Acknowledgments

The American Historical Association is grateful to the Mellon Foundation for its generous funding of the History Gateways initiative. The John N. Gardner Institute for Excellence in Undergraduate Education, especially Andrew K. Koch and Stephanie M. Foote, have been generous partners in this project. The backbone of this initiative was the faculty and administrators at our 11 participating institutions, whom the AHA thanks for their contributions.

The AHA also thanks advisors to the initiative, including Lou Albert, Michelle Alvarez, Bob Bain, John Bezis-Selfa, Kevin Brown, Lendol Calder, Ethan Campbell, Brent Drake, Jayme Feagin, Peter Felten, Trevor Getz, Trinidad Gonzales, David Graham, Betsy Griffin, Jennifer Hart, Resche Hines, Jeff Janowick, Norman Jones, Roberta Matthews, Vicki McGillin, Susannah McGowan, Daniel McInerney, Steven Mintz, Nancy Quam-Wickham, Matt Redinger, Robert Rodier, Sara Stein Koch, Heather Streets-Salter, Colleen Vasconcellos, Molly Warsh, Laura Westhoff, and Sam Wineburg.

The AHA Council, especially its Teaching Division, has supported this work. Thank you to Jennifer Baniewicz, Shannon Bontrager, Jeffrey Bowman, Carlos Contreras, Kathleen Hilliard, Alexandra Hui, Anne Hyde, Jacqueline Jones, Elizabeth Lehfeldt, Katharina Matro, Karen Marrero, Laura McEnaney, John McNeill, Edward Muir, Mary Beth Norton, Craig Perrier, Kenneth Pomeranz, James H. Sweet, and Charles Zappia.

We also acknowledge the invaluable contributions of former AHA staff members Emily Swafford, Megan Connor, and Claire Vanderwood.